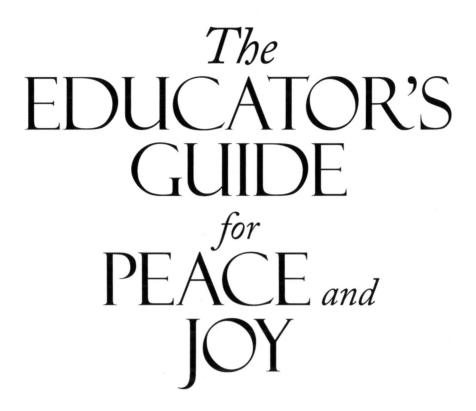

The EDUCATOR'S GUIDE *for* PEACE *and* JOY

AN ALPHABET OF STRATEGIES TO HELP YOU LIGHT YOUR INNER CANDLE

Elevate, Practice, Reflect, Discover

Gerry Fitzpatrick-Doria & Lauren Yack

BALBOA.PRESS
A DIVISION OF HAY HOUSE

Balboa Press books may be ordered through booksellers or by contacting:

Balboa Press
A Division of Hay House
1663 Liberty Drive
Bloomington, IN 47403
www.balboapress.com
844-682-1282

ISBN: 978-1-9822-6592-2 (sc)
ISBN: 978-1-9822-6593-9 (e)

Library of Congress Control Number: 2021906087

Print information available on the last page.

Balboa Press rev. date: 02/07/2022

Contents

Introduction

One day, Gerry, a new principal in Southwest Philadelphia, walked into a first-grade classroom where students had staged a true revolt. These first graders were frustrated with their teacher, and their teacher was equally frustrated with them. Students had overturned every single desk in the room and dumped the entire contents of their desks on the floor. All Gerry could see was a sea of papers, crayons, pencils, and books. The classroom was eerily quiet, and everyone stood still looking back at Gerry. The teacher and the students alike appeared defeated; they all knew that something had to change, but they just were not sure what to do. Do you ever feel so hopeless that you want to dump everything on the floor because you just can't take it any longer? Do you feel like something has to *shift*, but you are not quite sure how to begin? That day in the classroom, Gerry vowed to figure out how to help.

The Educator's Guide for Peace and Joy: An Alphabet of Strategies to Help You Light Your Inner Candle provides educators with a myriad of strategies to regain peace so they can light their inner candle. Educators cannot light and inspire others unless their own flames burn brightly. This guide to a living practice helps educators be the change they want to see in their classrooms and in their own lives. The strategies, practices, and ideas in this book help educators feel in tune with the meaning of their work by *shifting* the way they see their lives.

Most educators stay with a full classroom of students all day long. They are the facilitators of the climate and culture of the group. For the day to be successful, educators must do more than just plan the lessons, activities, and experiences. They must plan to be the light and inspiration for their students. This light must last all day, every day, for at least 180 days. According to Riser-Kositsky (2021) for the National Center for Educational Statistics, the total number of K–12 teachers in 2016 was 3.6 million. That number has decreased with the total number now being 3.2 million in the fall of 2021.

Currently, 90 percent of available teaching positions have been created by teachers who have left the position. Some teachers are retiring, but nearly two-thirds of these teachers have left for other reasons including connection to unhappiness, disappointment with the experience, stress, and working conditions (Carver-Thomas and Darling-Hammond 2017). Teachers are more stressed out at work than average people. Studies suggest that teachers and school staff are significantly more stressed than other US workers. Additionally, teachers reported experiences of poor mental health for eleven or more days each month. This rate is twice that of the general US workforce (American Federation of Teachers & BATs 2017). In addition, compared to education systems in other higher-achieving countries, US educators have a lower number of hours set aside for instructional planning, above-average class sizes, and more low-income students (Organization for Economic Co-operation and Development 2017).

More than ever before, educators are under a great deal of pressure. First, educators face the expectation that they will create conditions that meet the social and emotional needs of each child. To do that every day, educators have to figure out where each student is and what each student needs. How can they inspire if they are not inspired? Another pressure is standardized testing and the myriad of data points and achievement levels students must meet throughout the school year. Educators face pressure to ensure that each student grows socially and academically. Their yearly evaluations are impacted by their class' scores and by the scores of the entire school building. Educators also face growing external pressures such as the rash of school shootings across the country, the challenges with hate crimes, the rise of students with social and emotional concerns, and the onset of challenges that have surfaced around social media. The COVID-19 pandemic has added more fuel to a fire that had already been started.

Every one of these challenges, along with many more, can have a direct emotional effect upon the teacher's classroom and their life. Educators feel the fallout at a palpable level. Educators want every student to feel safe, to feel happy, and to learn. These high expectations place educators under constant pressure all day long. Educators are responsible for the daily encounters and the yearlong academic success of the students they serve. We need to inspire, empower, and reignite over three million educators. Imagine the possibilities that can occur for our students, their families, their communities, our nation, and our world when we are all coexisting at a high frequency. Right here, right now, we have the power to change the world.

As an experienced educational leader, Dr. Gerry Fitzpatrick-Doria has practiced and shared techniques that have allowed her to effectively manage her busy career and guide teachers and colleagues. During the summer following a traumatic school year, Gerry spent a few days alone at the beach. There, Gerry remembered all she knew to be true and renewed her practices of self-care and mindfulness. Gerry rekindled her own light and found joy again. She declared the next school year would be her year of self-care. Gerry began living these strategies: focusing on love over fear; gratitude; forgiveness; mindfulness; intentionality in thought and action; and finding the space and time for excitement and joy. Come the fall, many people commented on how Gerry appeared to be different and they asked her what had changed. For those who asked, she began to share her strategies, beliefs, ideas, and practices. Gerry lives by the words of Gandhi, "Be the light you want to see in the world." Thus, this book was born! *The Educator's Guide for Peace and Joy* helps educators light their own candle so that they can light the candles of others in their lives, whether they are students, colleagues, family, or friends. This soul book will help educators reflect, recharge, and rekindle their lights.

Gerry started the path to this book on her own. She then began having deep conversations with a friend and colleague, Lauren Yack. Gerry and Lauren first met during Gerry's first year as a principal. When Gerry arrived at the building, she was informed that the school district had just hired a new counselor for the building. This was Lauren's first year as a school counselor and she was amazing! Their partnership, friendship, and lifelong relationship began at that moment and grows stronger every day. Lauren's experience provides a supportive lens to this most important work. Lauren has been in K–12 education for nearly fifteen years. She has touched the lives of students, faculty, staff, and families in authentic and unique ways. Her experiences range from individual student support to elementary and high school counseling services. Lauren is steeped in research, analysis, and professional learning with strong focus on applied behavior analysis and trauma-informed care. With her myriad of experiences, extensive knowledge, and passion to lead from the heart, Lauren accepted the offer to join Gerry in providing this most important message to educators.

This book stands out from all the other solutions being served up to educators. Other books for educators focus on helping the teacher be a better teacher by gaining more pedagogical knowledge or specific strategies to use with their students. Those books are most important for the educator to continue to develop their professional practice, but they aren't everything the teacher needs. Teachers need a book for the soul. The International Council on Active Aging (n.d.) has identified seven dimensions of wellness: intellectual, physical, social, spiritual, vocational, emotional and environmental. All of these dimensions are addressed through specific strategies and resources.

The Educator's Guide for Peace and Joy meets educators at any stage of life. It is for new, emerging, and experienced educators who, in their hearts, believe there is a better way to live. It is for the educators who are giving everything they have to their students and must then rally energy and excitement so they can give everything they have to their families and personal commitments. It is for the educators who care deeply for the students and families they serve, and who are feeling depleted. It is for the educators who are extremely tired and who are trying to find balance and free themselves from the guilt of not being able to do it all. It is also for the educators who are already fired up, passionate, and excited about teaching and learning and who want to stay that way. Educators who are entering the last chapter of their careers may need a rekindling of their flames. Research has shown that programs for workplace wellness, mindfulness, social and emotional learning, and other types of support have been proven to improve educators' well-being. They have also found that through these practices also improve student outcomes (Greenberg, Brown, and Abenavoli 2016).

Many courageous teachers have shared their underlying fear that they are not good enough, skilled enough, or prepared enough to handle the current challenges. They also have shared that when they excel beyond measure, their colleagues sometimes treat them differently. We can help our educators *shift* their thinking. This inspiring quote by Marianne Williamson provides a springboard toward believing in ourselves, especially during these challenging times:

> Our deepest fear is not that we are inadequate. Our deepest fear is that we are powerful beyond measure. It is our light, not our darkness that most frightens us. We ask ourselves, "Who am I to be brilliant, gorgeous, talented, fabulous?" Actually, who are you not to be? Your playing small does not serve the world. There is nothing enlightened about shrinking so that other people won't feel insecure around you. We are all meant to shine, as children do. We were born to make manifest that which is within us. It's not just in some of us; it's in everyone. And as we let our own light shine, we unconsciously give other people permission to do the same. As we are liberated from our own fear, our presence automatically liberates others.

With *The Educator's Guide for Peace and Joy*, you can be the change. When you cultivate ways to keep your inner candle lit, you can *shift* in an instant. When your candle burns brightly, you have the strength and the power to be your best self and to use your flame to light the candles of others. Your flame, your light, your spark. You are power. The possibilities are unlimited. This easy-to-follow personal soul book can *shift* thoughts, *shift* actions, and *shift* lives. These are practices to last a lifetime and practices we encourage you to share with others.

How to Use This Guide

The Educator's Guide for Peace and Joy: An Alphabet of Strategies to Help You Light Your Inner Candle is an empowering book that educators can live in. It uses the twenty-six letters in the alphabet to create every word we read, speak, think, and write. *The Educator's Guide for Peace and Joy* soul book is built around twenty-six strategies, just as our entire language is built around twenty-six letters.

Each chapter focuses on one strategy, practice, or idea specifically connected to one letter of the alphabet. Each chapter is a two-page spread that you can live in. This format creates the conditions for you to intentionally commit to a practice and process that is both authentic and realistic. There are four sections to each chapter. The sections are **Elevate, Practice, Reflect,** and **Discover**. The **Elevate** quadrant connects you with the inspiration for the strategy and sets the tone for the self-work. The **Practice** quadrant provides you with the actual strategy and information to utilize in your daily life. These strategies typically do not cost you anything. Everything you need, you already have tucked inside your own brilliance. The **Reflect** quadrant gives you an opportunity to go within and internalize this practice and make it your own. This is very personal, individual, and authentic. The Reflect quadrant makes the book unique, differentiated, and special to each and every reader. No two reflections will ever be exactly the same, just as no two educators are ever the same. This section includes guided writing prompts and some space for reflective journaling. The last quadrant is **Discover**. This quadrant provides you with additional resources connected to the topic.

This book can be read and used in many different ways. You can take one chapter or strategy and focus on that for two weeks. With twenty-six strategies, this book can stretch over one year, which reinforces the learning and the practice. Or you can take a more accelerated approach by using a weekly strategy and completing a round of practice in six months. An even more accelerated practice would be to follow one strategy per day, allowing you to complete a round of practice in less than one month. To complete a round of the book, the chapters can be read in sequential order, yet they most certainly do not have to be read that way. You can choose your own unique order of the chapters. Additionally, this soul book can be read, reviewed, and reflected upon many, many times. The power is in the process. Sometimes in our lives we have to see, hear, or practice something multiple times before we make the heartfelt connection to it and before our internal *shift* occurs. Now is the time to kindle or rekindle your flame!

A Long-Term Resource for Educators

The Educator's Guide for Peace and Joy: An Alphabet of Strategies to Help You Light Your Inner Candle is for each and every one of the educators out there. The mounting concerns about health, safety, violence, student trauma, test scores, and increasing job responsibilities threaten to dominate our daily lives. Whether you are a novice or a seasoned professional, *The Educator's Guide for Peace and Joy* rises to meet you where you are. As a novice teacher, you may be just setting up your classroom, strategies, philosophies, and lifestyle. Using this book as a proactive measure, you can prepare for the busy days and years to come. As a seasoned teacher, you have been teaching for a while and might have been burning your candle at both ends by raising or caring for a family while teaching class after class, year after year. Using this book as a self-care measure, you can take the time to reflect and learn strategies to rekindle your flame. As a teacher with some years under your belt, you have some experience to draw from but are still learning and growing as a professional. You are beginning to make adjustments to your teaching style or philosophy, and you are beginning to see firsthand the challenges that educators face daily. Using this book as both a proactive and self-care measure, you can prepare for the future while learning and practicing strategies to help with the present.

Where do we look for answers? More and more research highlights the importance of a holistic approach to stress at the individual level. Many of these research studies advocate for future research about how to provide teachers with professional development training that will improve their coping skills. Here is where *The Educator's Guide for Peace and Joy: An Alphabet of Strategies to Help You Light Your Inner Candle* enters as a resource—both as a practical and compassionate support for all educators and as a professional development offering for schools and districts to support their teachers. Many of the strategies that researchers have identified as solutions are highlighted in this book; this book expands beyond those lists with more resources and support tailored for teachers to use long-term.

Elevate Quotes

The personalized and special quotes that open each chapter have their own story. Originally, Dr. Gerry Fitzpatrick-Doria selected a well-known quote to match each chapter, and somehow they didn't feel right. Gerry trashed them. The second time, Gerry pulled out all of her favorite books and resources and chose a quote for each chapter from her favorite authors and leaders. That still didn't feel right. Gerry trashed that batch as well. Finally, while sitting quietly in meditation, the answer came to her. Gerry reached out to authentic women and men who have dramatically touched her life and asked them for a quote. Just like Goldilocks found the "just right" chair, the "just right" quotes were found. They have been written specifically for YOU! Deep gratitude is offered to all those who have taken the time to craft a quote and to all who have taken the time to read them. Let's celebrate the fact that we continue to build and grow our community.

Chapter 1
Awareness

ELEVATE

It's because you shine so bright … some fear that you will expose the darkness
that resides inside of themselves. Don't dim yourself down, keep shining!
—Elizabeth Lindsay, *Angel with an Edge*

PRACTICE

Awareness is the knowledge or perception of a situation or fact in our current "now" moment. A great way for us to find our "now" moment is to look down at our feet. Where are we right now? This is our "now" moment. You have chosen to read this book, and you are aware that either your light needs to be rekindled or you want to ensure that your light continues to shine brightly each and every day. You realize that you want to ensure that your inner candle is strong so that you can live your best life possible. You are aware that there are a finite number of minutes in each day, and that being in the present moment and taking care of yourself will change the world. You will feel better, and then you will be able to light or reignite the candles of others.

Awareness, as a practice, is the intentionality of being in the present moment. Being aware of where we are in each present moment is powerful! We are so often in a moment of time and thinking about the next moment in time. An example of this is having the opportunity to sit down and eat a meal, and instead of enjoying the food that has been prepared, we eat it quickly because we feel we have to make a phone call or read our email or toss a pile of dirty clothes into the washing machine. Unfortunately, distractions rob us of our awareness of the present moment.

Awareness also supports us in checking in with ourselves to see how we are feeling. Our feelings offer us great guidance. An excellent practice of awareness is to check in on how we are feeling. If we are feeling calm, steady, joyful, loving, and peaceful, we can smile to confirm we are on point. If we are feeling anxious, stressed, agitated, or uncomfortable, this practice of awareness will let us know where we are, and then we can intentionally *shift* our attention to find some good in the situation. If we realize that we are feeling anxious because we feel we don't have enough time to complete a task, we can recognize and celebrate what we have done thus far and tell ourselves that in this present moment in time all is well.

We can quickly check ourselves by assessing how we feel. Let's take a moment to check in right now. Take a long, deep breath. Hold the breath and count to five in your head. Now let it out. Check in on yourself to identify how you feel. Only you really know. I feel _____. It can range from horrible to fabulous. Many of us do a check-in with our students each day by asking the question, "How are you feeling, on a scale of zero to five? Zero means let's call 911, and five is fantastic." Knowing where we are socially, emotionally, mentally, and spiritually is important information that we can use to decide if we want to stay where we are or try to make some improvements.

Practice Reminder: "Today I will …"

Chapter 1
Awareness

REFLECT

Here you have an opportunity to take some time and think about awareness. You may find it beneficial to write out your responses.

- ❖ This chapter's Elevate quote is directly aligned to awareness. Take a moment and read the quote aloud to yourself. See, hear, and feel the words. What resonates with you?
- ❖ How am I feeling right now?
- ❖ If I find myself in a place where I'm not feeling well or not thinking positive thoughts, will I choose to *shift* my perspective?
- ❖ Finish the phrase: "And the good news is _____."
- ❖ If this doesn't work for me, what might my authentic phrase be that will *shift* my perspective from negative to positive or bring my awareness to the present moment?
- ❖ Am I aware of the bright light that is inside me at all times?
- ❖ Can I find opportunities to share the importance of becoming aware with others?

DISCOVER

If you want to explore this topic further, check out the resources below.

People:

- Thich Nhat Hanh, Revered Zen Teacher: https://plumvillage.org/
- Dr. Christine Kiesinger
  Facebook: https://www.facebook.com/christine.kiesinger
  LinkedIn: https://www.linkedin.com/in/christine-kiesinger-ph-d-4034664/
- Elizabeth Lindsay, Angels with an Edge: https://angelwithanedge.com/about/elizabeth-lindsay/

Places:

- Studio Be: https://www.studiobemindfulness.com/
- Awakin.org: https://www.awakin.org/read/, weekly recommended reading to encourage and facilitate insight and reflection
- Jersey Shore Mindfulness: http://www.jerseyshoremindfulness.com/
- Mindful Awareness Research Center: https://www.uclahealth.org/marc/

Things:

- *The Miracle of Mindfulness* by Thich Nhat Hanh
- *Happy Teachers Change the World* by Thich Nhat Hanh
- *Gift From the Sea* by Anne Morrow Lindbergh
- "The Power of Vulnerability," https://peak-careers.com/ted-talks-self-care/

Chapter 2
Breath

ELEVATE

Your breath is the sustenance of life…something that never ends, until it is your last…
Breathing is a physical and emotional experience and one of life's most precious
gifts…As your breath ebbs and flows like the tides, your connection to the dance
of movement allows you to have complete control of your mind and body.
—Joyce Trantas Gutchigian, educator

PRACTICE

Scuba divers are trained to regulate their breathing. It is a physical fact that when divers are anxious, their breathing becomes quick and shallow. This type of breathing is not good for the body, nor is it good for the scuba diver. When breathing quickly, the diver uses up the air in the tank far too quickly. Fast, shallow breathing is not good for the educator either. When you breathe in a shallow fashion, your body remains in a cyclical state of stress. This type of shallow breathing can become a habit. Your cortisol may be rising dramatically. Cortisol is not a friend to peace and joy. Educators can be intentional in using their breath to create an atmosphere of peace at any and every moment. Here are a few guided breathing techniques to place in your tool kit to use whenever needed.

Let's try one of the following breathing exercises.

1. Place your awareness on your breath. You can do this anywhere and at any time. Intentionally breathe in, intentionally breathe out, and sit there for a moment. You can do this with your eyes open or closed.

2. Place one hand or both hands on your heart. You can be seated or standing. Your eyes can be open or closed. Feel your heart beating and begin breathing in and out with a rhythm that feels right to you. You may want to let your shoulders drop and place a smile on your face.

3. Place yourself in a comfortable seated position with both feet flat on the floor. Straighten your spine. Place your hands on your thighs. Close your eyes. Take a long, deep breath in through your nose, filling your lungs to capacity. Silently count to seven. Now exhale through your mouth, making sure to let as much air out as possible. Pace your breath by mentally counting to seven during your exhale as well. Repeat this process several times.

Practice Reminder: "Today I will …"

Chapter 2
Breath

REFLECT

Here you have an opportunity to take some time and think about breath. You may find it beneficial to write out your responses.

- ❖ This chapter's Elevate quote is directly aligned to breath. Take a moment and read the quote aloud to yourself. See, hear, and feel the words. What resonates with you?
- ❖ Do I feel as though I am grasping for breath, both figuratively and literally? Is everything racing by so quickly in my classroom and in my life that I feel like there is not enough time or air in my space?
- ❖ Which breathing technique did I try? How did it feel?
- ❖ What did I like about this technique? Why?
- ❖ What did I dislike about this technique? Why?
- ❖ Can I see myself using this technique in a stressful moment? If yes, where?
- ❖ Can I find opportunities to share the importance of intentionally using my breath with others?

DISCOVER

If you want to explore this topic further, check out the resources below.

Places:

- Headspace website and app: https://www.headspace.com/meditation/breathing-exercises
- Heart Math Institute: https://www.heartmath.org
- Breathe for Change: https://www.breatheforchange.com/
- Gaiam Blog: https://www.gaiam.com/blogs/discover

Things:

- "Three Breathing Exercises And Techniques," https://www.drweil.com/health-wellness/body-mind-spirit/stress-anxiety/breathing-three-exercises/
- "Greater Good in Action: Mindful Breathing," https://ggia.berkeley.edu/practice/mindful_breathing
- "Mindful: A Guided Meditation to Encourage Deep Breathing," https://www.mindful.org/a-guided-meditation-to-encourage-deep-breathing/
- "Mindful Breathing Meditation," https://www.youtube.com/watch?v=nmFUDkj1Aq0
- "Listening Meditation for Grounding," https://www.youtube.com/watch?v=c2thahBgErc&feature=emb_rel_pause
- "Change your Breath, Change your Life," https://www.youtube.com/watch?v=_QTJOAI0UoU&feature=share&fbclid=IwAR1h4NRNck0oNO_0wwfH9WndBzeitWo--9lADOLGLEE178tn700-aR295dM
- "How To Perform the 4-7-8 Breathing Exercise" by Andrew Weil, MD, https://www.youtube.com/watch?v=YRPh_GaiL8s
- "How to Meditate," https://www.mindful.org/how-to-meditate/
- "Meditation for Beginners," https://www.headspace.com/meditation/meditation-for-beginners
- "Meditation: A Simple and Fast Way to Reduce Stress," https://www.mayoclinic.org/tests-procedures/meditation/in-depth/meditation/art-20045858

Chapter 3
Choose Your Words Carefully

ELEVATE

> Let your words be the spark that sets your soul on fire.
> —Shareese Barnett Nelson, vice principal

PRACTICE

The words we think and the words we speak create our lives. Take a mental snapshot of your current life—what you look like, where you live, what's in your bank account, who you associate with, and where you go. Everything started as a word in your head. Each one of us is responsible for our "right now" experience.

At first blush, this might sound a tad off-putting. The great news is that our current thoughts are creating our future experiences. Have you ever thought to yourself, *Why is* this *happening to me?* The "this" can be a good thing or a not-so-good thing. The "this" can be something that's happening in your classroom, in your school, or in your personal life. The answer is as simple and as powerful as your very own words. You have the unlimited and uncompromising power to change your world. Yes, this *shift* can occur through the intentionality of the words you choose. The words we choose to use in our lives create our future chapters and situations. Where we are currently is in direct connection to the words we have used in the past. Now that you know the power of words, I'm sure you want to fine-tune your craft of using them.

Try to pay attention to your thoughts and your words. When you look in a mirror, what do you think or say to yourself? When you check your bank balance, what do you think or say to yourself? When you make a mistake, what do you think or say to yourself? What we think and say about ourselves creates our life. Try to pay attention without feeling guilt! Listen to your thoughts and words. Take note of any patterns or name-calling that surfaces. Many people think or say negative things about themselves like, *I'm stupid, I'm fat, I'm broke, I'm sick, I'm clumsy,* and so on. Now, we are asking you to SHIFT your thinking. If our thoughts create our life (and they do), then let's create a positive one. You can make this playful and have fun with it. We would even encourage you to never take a "sick day" again; if you must call out, we encourage you to take a "day of healing"

This is about identifying where we are and *shifting* our perspective. Our practice here is to catch ourselves when we think or speak words that define the opposite of what we want. When practicing our awareness (see Chapter 1) and checking in, we have to really listen and hear the words we speak about ourselves, our lives, and our future. We will practice noticing and *shifting*, when appropriate. Here are some examples:

I thought: Dang it, I'm always late to everything. I *shifted* to: I'm beginning to show up on time more and more.

I said: I have a headache. I *shifted* to: I'm already healing, and I'm happy that I can still help my daughter with her homework.

I thought: I'm tired all the time. I *shifted* to: I am so grateful when I can celebrate my moments of energy.

I thought: I hate paying the bills because I'm always broke. I *shifted* to: I'm so grateful that I have a good job and I can pay this bill right here.

Practice Reminder: "Today I will …"

Chapter 3
Choose Your Words Carefully

REFLECT

Here you have an opportunity to take some time and think about word choice. You may find it beneficial to write out your responses.

- ❖ This chapter's Elevate quote is directly aligned to word choice. Take a moment and read the quote aloud to yourself. See, hear, and feel the words. What resonates with you?
- ❖ During my first day of practice, when I was just noticing my thoughts and words, what showed up that I didn't expect?
- ❖ When have I had a desired outcome that I can link directly to something positive I have said? When have I had an undesired outcome that I can link directly to something negative I have said?
- ❖ Am I aware of how I feel when I say things about myself or others?
- ❖ Can I find opportunities to share with others about the importance of choosing our words carefully?

DISCOVER

If you want to explore this topic further, check out the resources below.

People:

- • Louise Hay, founder of Hay House: https://www.louisehay.com/honoring-louises-you-can-heal-your-life-legacy/
- • Denise Linn, current Spiritual Leader: http://www.deniselinn.com/

Things:

- • *You Can Heal Your Life* by Louise Hay
- • *What to Say When You Talk to Yourself* by Shad Helmstetter, Ph.D.
- • "Positive thinking: Stop negative self-talk to reduce stress," https://www.mayoclinic.org/healthy-lifestyle/stress-management/in-depth/positive-thinking/art-20043950
- • "The power of positive self-talk," https://mylearningnetwork.com/the-power-of-positive-self-talk/
- • "6 Ways to Become More Positive Today," https://www.psychologytoday.com/us/blog/hope-relationships/201409/6-ways-become-more-positive-today

Chapter 4
Decision-Making

ELEVATE

> Don't allow fear to let you think that you have made a wrong decision, for
> there are no wrong decisions. Don't allow fear to make you think that you have
> made a mistake, for there are no mistakes. You must begin to feel fear as soon
> as it arrives, so that you can acknowledge it and then send it on its way!
> —Laura Bushnell, author

PRACTICE

The average teacher makes 1,500 educational decisions every school day. This boils down to four educational decisions per minute, which is one educational decision every fifteen seconds. Couple this with the decisions the average teacher makes in their personal life and it can make your head spin (TeachThought Staff, 2019).

Have you ever felt in a panic when you have to make a decision? Tierney (2011) wrote about decision fatigue in the *New York Times*. They shared that when you make decision after decision, both in your personal and professional life, this eventually results in diminished energy, or fatigue, to continue making decisions that are rational. This lack of energy to make rational decisions causes one of two outcomes: you either act impulsively or you do nothing. Acting impulsively can leave you with something that you don't want or need, and you might feel frustrated or stupid. That frozen feeling, the "do nothing" outcome, can leave you with bigger problems in the future and can leave you feeling frustrated or helpless.

Being able to make a decision and feel confident in that decision provides an authentic level of peace. Applying intentional approaches to decision-making can help in the moment when making the decision and while living with the decision in the future. The good news is that we already have the answers we need inside of us. When you come up against a challenge, place your hand on your heart and take a few deep breaths (see Chapter 2). When we take time and be still, even if that time is only a few moments, what we need to do or what we need to say will most certainly surface. Action that is directly connected to your soul and your authentic passion! When tasked with making a decision, below are some questions that can guide you.

1. What about *this* aligns with my core values?

2. As I prioritize my life, does *this* live on the top of my list?

3. When I think about *this* do I feel joyful?

4. How much time will *this* take?

5. Is there something or someone that can inform my decision?

Practice Reminder: "Today I will …"

Chapter 4
Decision-Making

REFLECT

Here you have an opportunity to take some time and think about decision-making. You may find it beneficial to write out your responses.

- ❖ This chapter's Elevate quote is directly aligned to decision-making. Take a moment and read the quote aloud to yourself. See, hear, and feel the words. What resonates with you?
- ❖ What bold decision could I, or did I, make? How did this make me feel?
- ❖ What action did I consider taking or actually take? How did this make me feel?
- ❖ Think of a recent problem in my life … How did I solve it? What decision did I make? Did other peoples' thoughts, opinions, and/or actions impact my decision?
- ❖ If I could have a "do-over," would I make the same decision again?
  - ➢ If yes, why?
  - ➢ If no, what would I do differently?
- ❖ Can I find opportunities to share the importance of intentional decision-making with others?

DISCOVER

If you want to explore this topic further, check out the resources below.

Places:

- Living Peace Institute: https://www.livingpeaceinstitute.com/?fbclid= IwAR2JTlhsLSzOCrDNFEFaFMKA0VtcnX312Yn1F48qWCN2wLPdjkaYHSeDzDM

Things:

- "MindTools: How to Make Decisions," https://www.mindtools.com/pages/article/ newTED_00.htm
- "Harvard Business Review: The Effective Decision," https://hbr.org/1967/01/ the-effective-decision
- Thompson-Grove (2004, revised 2012), "What? So What? Now What?", School Reform Initiative (SRI): A Community of Learners, http://schoolreforminitiative.org/doc/what_ so_what.pdf
- Tierney, John. (2011) Do You Suffer From Decision Fatigue? Retrieved from: https:// www.nytimes.com/2011/08/21/magazine/do-you-suffer-from-decision-fatigue.html

Chapter 5
Energy

ELEVATE

The Universe loves us and wants us to have what it is we desire. Too many of us focus on what we don't have, and this is the energy that expands. The Universe only responds to our energy, so if lack is where we are, it shows up as more lack. But, if you can *shift* into abundance and gratitude, the Universe brings you more of that. We are co-creators with the Universe in what happens in our lives. We have so much more power than we realize. When you believe in magic, magical things happen.
—Melisa Caprio, *Postcards to the Universe*

PRACTICE

As a principal, Gerry remembers a time when she walked into a classroom and no one even noticed she was there. The educator was sitting with a small group of children. They were talking and laughing about the book in front of them. The other students were scattered about the classroom. Some were working independently and others were working in pairs or triads. The students were engaged and smiling. You could feel the love of learning and the respect toward each other.

Just as we can feel the positive, sometimes we walk into a negative space. Have you walked into a classroom, a teacher's lounge, or in your own home after an argument took place and you could feel the negativity? You cannot see it, but you can feel it. In the same thinking, have you ever walked into a classroom and you can feel the love and kindness? You can feel the vibe, the vibrations. All of this is energy!

Let's try a positive energy game. This will help you travel through the day energetically, positively, and joyously. Here's how to play: First, pay attention to who or what aggravates you, then flip the switch. At that moment, when you recognize the annoyance, the aggravation, or the dislike, flip the switch and *shift* your thinking to find something positive about that person or situation. Toss away the crappy feelings and negative thoughts or comments about others and replace them with love. You are in control!

An unknown author stated, "Your energy introduces you before you even speak." Just because you can't see something doesn't mean it's not there; energy is everywhere. What we think about and speak about comes about. Let's *shift* our energy!

Practice Reminder: "Today I will …"

Chapter 5
Energy

REFLECT

Here you have an opportunity to take some time and think about energy. You may find it beneficial to write out your responses.

- ❖ This chapter's Elevate quote is directly aligned to energy. Take a moment and read the quote aloud to yourself. See, hear, and feel the words. What resonates with you?
- ❖ Think about or describe a time when I walked into a room and felt positive or negative energy.
  - ➢ What had happened before, during, and after?
  - ➢ Did the energy in the room change my energy?
- ❖ Can I find opportunities to share the importance of our energy with others?

DISCOVER

If you want to explore this topic further, check out the resources below.

People:

- Pam Grout - https://pamgrout.com/
- Linda Elliott, Energy Work Practitioner https://soulutionsfordailyliving.com/linda-elliott/
- Jaime Pfeffer - jaimepfeffer.com
  - o Shop (including guided meditations): jaimepfeffer.com/shop
  - o Free psychic readings on YouTube: bit.ly/JaimePYT
  - o Facebook business page: bit.ly/jaimepfacebook
  - o Pinterest: bit.ly/JaimePinteres

Places:

- Soulutions for Daily Living: https://soulutionsfordailyliving.com/?fbclid=IwAR3dHC qbngSco2l7sq4bmld98zIxUe_1OQXZZR8NS8bY04kRy2hHaL_9psI
- Postcards to the Universe: https://www.postcardstotheuniverse.com/?fbclid= IwAR1nEQMtyK50hPoMAaXe2LLiSwFspxlcASkDmLz0T5jLF4UJ56sAfR3wCgI

Things:

- *E-Squared* by Pam Grout
- "Using Daily Feelings Check-In," https://www.socialemotionalworkshop.com/2019/12/ feelings-check-in/

Chapter 6
Forgiveness

ELEVATE

> Never regret being a nice person to another human being. Your kindness is karmic
> and says everything about you. Their behavior says everything about them. What
> comes out of a person belongs to them. How they treat you tells you everything you
> need to know. Respect yourself to love yourself most. If you have to walk away it's
> okay. In the end it's between you and Spirit. It's never between you and them.
> —Elizabeth Lindsay, *Angel with an Edge*

PRACTICE

Every day Gerry wears a silver pinkie ring. It is shaped like a key. Gerry wears this ring purposely every single day to remind herself to forgive and to offer forgiveness to herself and to others all day long. If someone aggravates her, talks about her actions, or is rude to her, she looks down to the ring and reminds herself to forgive. Forgiveness is a gift to self. Let's imagine we are carrying a backpack. Every time someone annoys or angers us, we will place a stone in the backpack and keep it there until we forgive the person. The more stones we have in our backpack, the heavier the load becomes. If we carry resentment, it is bothersome to us and not to the other person. Small annoyances and aggravations can occur all day long in a classroom setting. Each student comes into the classroom with their personality and their fears, just as educators do. Grievances can be big or small. It does not matter their size; their power to impact your day is the same.

Below are sample techniques to practice when forgiveness feels difficult or impossible.

1. **Sympathy for the person you are trying to forgive**
   Sometimes it is really difficult to put yourself in another's shoes when they have wronged you or hurt you in a serious way. Instead of empathy, try to feel sympathy for the person (Souders, 2019).
2. **Self-soothing**
   You cannot undo the harm, irritation, or anger you felt in that moment or situation but you can try to control it. Try strategies to self-soothe, such as deep breathing, talking to a trusted person, taking a walk, or going to a preferred place (Souders, 2019).
3. **Empty chair technique**
   Sit in a chair and place a second chair across from you or next to you. Imagine that the person who angered, annoyed, or hurt you is sitting in that chair. Tell the person, as if they were sitting in that chair, about your complaint or problem and how you feel. Then move to the empty chair and pretend you are the person you are trying to forgive. Respond to what you said from that person's perspective. Go back and forth between the two chairs as many times as needed (Souders, 2019).
4. **Give blessings today**
   It is essential to use this idea if anyone seems to cause an adverse reaction in us. We can offer that person the blessing of our holiness immediately (by sharing our light), so that we may learn to keep it in our own awareness, grounded in love and peace. For me, this is a perfect walking/living action, prayer, and meditation. This one action alone absolutely *shifts* my particular moment in time, then the next moment in time, and then the next, and so on. (Adapted from ACIM Workbook Lesson 37.)

Practice Reminder: "Today I will …"

Chapter 6
Forgiveness

REFLECT

Here you have an opportunity to take some time and think about forgiveness. You may find it beneficial to write out your responses.

- ❖ This chapter's Elevate quote is directly aligned to forgiveness. Take a moment and read the quote aloud to yourself. See, hear, and feel the words. What resonates with you?
- ❖ Can I remember a time when I gave or received forgiveness? Can I remember how that felt?
- ❖ Which technique do I think would be most effective for me?
  - ➤ What do I like about this technique? Why?
  - ➤ What do I dislike about this technique? Why?
- ❖ Can I see myself using this in the moment? If yes, where? Think of or share an example.
- ❖ Has a student, colleague, friend, or family member angered or agitated me today? How can I try forgiveness toward that person?
- ❖ Can I find opportunities to share the importance of forgiveness with others?

DISCOVER

If you want to explore this topic further, check out the resources below.

Places:

- Positive Psychology: www.positivepsychology.com
- International Forgiveness Institute: https://internationalforgiveness.wordpress.com/

Things:

- *Daring Greatly: How the Courage to Be Vulnerable Transforms the Way We Live* by Brene Brown
- Enright, Robert D.; Fitzgibbons, Richard P. (2015). Forgiveness therapy: An empirical guide for resolving anger and restoring hope.
- Chikako Ozawa-de Silva, Associate Professor of Anthropology on Naikan, which means "inner looking", a contemplative practice: https://vimeo.com/76080468 https://vimeo.com/75236784 https://vimeo.com/76063250
- "Forgiveness: Letting go of grudges and bitterness," https://www.mayoclinic.org/healthy-lifestyle/adult-health/in-depth/forgiveness/art-20047692
- "Let it Go 11 Ways to Forgive," https://www.mindful.org/let-go-11-ways-forgive/
- "The Power of Forgiveness," https://www.health.harvard.edu/mind-and-mood/the-power-of-forgiveness
- Toussaint, L., Kamble, S., Marschallm, J., & Duggi, D. (2016). The effects of brief prayer on the experience of forgiveness: An American and Indian comparison. Int J Psychol. 2016 Aug;51(4):288-95. doi: 10.1002/ijop.12139. Epub 2015 Jan 16.
- Souders, Beata (2019) - 8 Tips and Techniques for When It Feels Too Hard to Forgive Retrieved from: https://positivepsychology.com/forgiveness-exercises-tips-activities-worksheets/

Chapter 7
Gratitude

ELEVATE

Gratitude gives fresh eyes in which to see the world. I am grateful to be able to send light and love to all that I meet on my journey.
—Anne Marie H. Kuvik, educator

Gratitude is the feeling you get from deep appreciation; when you sit in wonder and awe of the sound of the birds, the crash of the ocean, or the smile of a beloved. Bask in it. It is the doorway to manifestation.
—Jennifer Grace, author, spiritual leader, and entrepreneur

PRACTICE

Every morning when Gerry gets out of bed, she gives thanks. When her first foot hits the floor, Gerry says, "Thank," and when her second foot hits the floor, she says, "You." Starting every day in gratitude sets Gerry up for a successful and positive day. Also, every month, when Gerry balances her bank statements and gets ready to pay her bills, she writes, "Thank You" at the top of her ledger.

Have you ever found yourself spending time and effort thinking about what you don't have, what is not working well for you, or what future events will eventually make you happy? These "I don't have _____" thoughts can occur at school or at home. We might see a colleague with a better caseload, classroom, or résumé. We may see a friend or family member with more money, more free time, or more friendships. Spending our important time and mind space thinking about what is *not* in our world is a huge waste of precious time. Celebrating what we currently have creates joy.

Let's explore and practice ways to identify all that we are grateful for in our lives and specifically in our current moments. The practice is simple. You can:

1. Create gratitude by filling a jar with slips of paper that describe things, experiences, and people you are grateful for;

2. Write what or who you are grateful for in a journal;

3. Share your gratitude with someone through a text, letter, or card;

4. Choose your own way to identify and/or share your gratitude.

If you ever have a day when you are finding it challenging to be thankful, read some of the slips or journal entries you have in your gratitude jar or journal to remind you.

Practice Reminder: "Today I will …"

Chapter 7
Gratitude

REFLECT

Here you have an opportunity to take some time and think about gratitude. You may find it beneficial to write out your responses.

❖ This chapter's Elevate quote is directly aligned to gratitude. Take a moment and read the quote aloud to yourself. See, hear, and feel the words. What resonates with you?

❖ When I am feeling frustrated, scared, or annoyed, am I willing to take a few breaths and identify five things that I'm grateful to have in my life? I can use my right hand to keep track. If my perspective hasn't yet *shifted*, am I willing to move to ten?

❖ Before moving forward in my day, I will try saying this: "I am grateful for _____." List everything that comes to mind.

❖ Repeat this affirmation of gratitude: "My heart is filled with gratitude for all the blessings in my life, and I celebrate who I am. I have much to be thankful for."

❖ Can I find opportunities to share the importance of gratitude with others?

DISCOVER

If you want to explore this topic further, check out the resources below.

Places:

• Go to https://positivepsychology.com/blog/ and use the Search tool to find these helpful articles:
  ○ 14 Health Benefits of Practicing Gratitude According to Science
  ○ The Science and Research on Gratitude and Happiness
  ○ The 34 Best TED Talks And Videos on the Power of Gratitude
  ○ The Gratitude Journal: Prompts, PDFs, and Worksheets
• Network for Grateful Living, https://gratefulness.org

Things:

• Emmons, R. A., and M. E. McCullough, eds. 2004. *The Psychology of Gratitude.* New York: Oxford Press. Unedited article: https://emmons.faculty.ucdavis.edu/wp-content/uploads/sites/90/2015/08/2011_2-16_Sheldon_Chapter-16-11.pdf
• Francis J. Flynn, "Frank Flynn: Gratitude, the Gift That Keeps on Giving," Stanford Graduate School of Business, March 1, 2012 https://www.gsb.stanford.edu/insights/frank-flynn-gratitude-gift-keeps-giving
• "Gratitude: The Short Film" by Louie Schwartzberg https://www.youtube.com/watch?v=cpkEvBtyL7M
• "The Evidence on Giving Thanks," https://www.psychologytoday.com/us/blog/evidence-based-living/201911/the-evidence-giving-thanks

Chapter 8
Hope

ELEVATE

When in darkness, hope will always BRIGHTEN your soul and your smile.
—Tamilla Mullings, author and businesswoman

PRACTICE

To be hopeful is to expect with confidence and to trust in the outcome. Here we are focusing on our thoughts and feelings, and the importance of placing our attention on what we want. As educators, we do this every day when we enter our classroom. Educators are most aware that every day is a new day. Our students might have done something yesterday that we wish they hadn't, yet we are able to start each day fresh and give each student the opportunity to try again and learn again. If Monday was not so good, we are most hopeful that Tuesday will be amazing. We give this to our students, families, and friends, but we also have to give this to ourselves.

We can tap into our level of hope by exploring some of our more challenging situations. These situations can be in class, at home, in our family, with our friends, or across our nation and the world. You can practice right now. Place your hand on your heart and take a few long cleansing breaths. You know how, as you have been doing this for a while. Now, close your eyes and think about something that's challenging to you right now. It can be personal or professional. Hold that thought then, regarding this specific situation, think about the best possible outcome. It may seem impossible, and that's okay. Think it anyway. Now take a step past thinking and move into feeling. What would it feel like to expect with confidence and to trust the best possible outcome? That's the feeling of hope. Sit with it for a while. You've got the power.

To practice and inspire hope, try creating a vision board around the concept of hope. You can focus on anything you choose. What does hope look like, feel like, sound like, etc.?

- Find or draw pictures that represent the feelings and experiences you want.
- Write inspirational quotes or personal anecdotes that move you or speak to you.
- Think about the feelings you want, the ones that make you feel good and most like you. Find or draw pictures that represent those feelings or write the feelings in words.
- Be selective; pick and choose what is most important to you!
- Keep it neat and simple.
- Have fun with this activity! (Canfield, 2017)

Practice Reminder: "Today I will …"

Chapter 8
Hope

REFLECT

Here you have an opportunity to take some time and think about hope. You may find it beneficial to write out your responses.

- ❖ This chapter's Elevate quote is directly aligned to hope. Take a moment and read the quote aloud to yourself. See, hear, and feel the words. What resonates with you?
- ❖ Did I make a vision board? If so, what did I focus on? What experiences and feelings did I include on my board?
  - ➢ If I did not make a vision board, why not?
- ❖ What are some areas in my life where hope rises?
  - ➢ How can I replicate that in other areas of my life?
- ❖ What are some areas in my life where being hopeful feels more challenging?
- ❖ Can I find opportunities to share the importance of hope with others?

DISCOVER

If you want to explore this topic further, check out the resources below.

People:

- Tamilla Mullings
  Instagram: www.instagram.com/becomingme15

Places:

- "Nurturing Hope" blog: https://blog.iqmatrix.com/nurturing-hope

Things:

- *Becoming Me* by Tamilla Mullings
- Jack Canfield - YouTube video about creating a vision board https://www.youtube.com/watch?v=iamZEW0x3dM
- "Finding Hope," https://www.psychologytoday.com/us/blog/pieces-mind/201504/finding-hope
- "27 Ways to Find HOPE: During Difficult Times," https://moorewellness.life/ways-find-hope/

Chapter 9
Inner Smile

ELEVATE

Smiles set miracles in motion!
—Larry Brown, educator

PRACTICE

The daily steps that we take to create our peaceful life are most certainly an inside job. We have the power to create so very much. The inspiration for this chapter and practice sprouted from a Taoist experience of the inner smile meditation. We will get to experience that in a bit, but for now, let's just play around with having an inner smile. Have you ever experienced the feeling of meeting someone on the street or in a store, someone whom you don't know, and you look at them and they smile at you? You can immediately feel the warmth and kindness coming from someone you don't even know. Oftentimes we immediately smile back, just like the reflection in a mirror. How about when you see a smiling baby? I dare you not to smile when you see a smiling baby. Just a quick connection with the smile of another can immediately *shift* our moment in time. Those external supports are wonderful and amazing.

The good news is that we have this power in our pocket at all times. We can create those feelings of peace, joy, love, and acceptance by creating that smile for ourselves. To practice, close your eyes and take a few deep breaths, then slowly place a smile on your face. You may need to think of something or someone to get you into a smiling mood, or you may be able to create that feeling on your own. Whatever it takes, do that. Once you get the feel for your inner smile you can begin to send this smile and peaceful energy to all parts of your body, both inside and out. Let's practice this for a moment. Close your eyes again. Take a few deep breaths. Plant that beautiful smile on your face. You can sit in this space for a moment. When you feel ready, you can begin to send this beautiful healing and peaceful smile throughout your body. You can send it to your heart, your organs, your blood stream, your muscles, your fingers, and your toes. You can send this beautiful smile wherever you choose. You are also invited to imagine that whatever your inner smile touches is either healed or recharged. There is no time limit on this, as you can spend the amount of time that feels right for you.

Smiling can reduce blood pressure, increase endurance, reduce pain and stress, and can boost the immune system. Who doesn't want a piece of that?

Practice Reminder: "Today I will …"

Chapter 9
Inner Smile

REFLECT

Here you have an opportunity to take some time and think about your inner smile. You may find it beneficial to write out your responses.

- ❖ This chapter's Elevate quote is directly aligned to your inner smile. Take a moment and read the quote aloud to yourself. See, hear, and feel the words. What resonates with you?
- ❖ How does my body feel when I have an inner smile?
- ❖ How can my inner smile affect others even if they can't see it?
- ❖ When I notice my inner smile, I am going to take time (however much I want or need to take) to immerse myself in it. How does that feel?
- ❖ Can I find opportunities to share the importance of smiling with others?

DISCOVER

If you want to explore this topic further, check out the resources below.

Places:

- • Tibetan Healing Sounds: Cleans the aura and removes all negative energy: https://www.youtube.com/watch?v=x6UITRjhijI

Things:

- • "Surprising Health Benefits Of Smiling" by Earlexia Norwood, MD, https://www.henryford.com/blog/2017/10/health-benefits-smiling
- • "How to Practice the 'Inner Smile' With Taoism," https://www.learnreligions.com/practice-the-inner-smile-3182953
- • "Enhance Your Health & Wellbeing With Inner Smile Meditation," https://insighttimer.com/blog/what-is-inner-smile-meditation/
- • "The Power of a Smile," http://yoffielife.com/power-smile/
- • "Inner Smile Meditation," https://www.youtube.com/watch?v=M7KtNrfgwjA
- • Dr. Deb Kern "Inner Smile Meditation" by Dr. Deb Kern, https://soundcloud.com/drdebkern/inner-smile-meditation

Chapter 10
Joy

ELEVATE

Joy is not 'an emotion' - Joy is a decision you make - it's a choice to be what you really are in truth. Joy is the result of knowing your oneness with everyone and everything. Joy is a vocation AND a vacation. It doesn't matter what the world does, it doesn't matter what the body does, it doesn't matter what other people do. Nothing can take your joy away, ever. Joy is IN YOU and all that is needed is to say: Yes. I am going to CONNECT WITH JOY and BE IT and BRING IT. Wherever you go, bring the joy! You'll see that you absolutely positively can bring joy and love into all the spaces you enter into, when you decide THAT'S WHAT I'M DOING. I'm bringing the joy, the love, the gratitude, the fun, the laughter, the presence of God.
—Lisa Natoli, spiritual leader, teacher, and author

PRACTICE

When times are tough or life is not meeting your expectations, it can be easy to respond with anger, disappointment, or hurt feelings. Finding joy can seem impossible. Just like we don't give up on our students, we can't give up on finding joy in hard times. Joy is all around us, but sometimes we have to use our awareness (see Chapter 1) to help us find it. One day, while Lauren was scrolling Facebook, a funny meme said, "Amazing things will happen today if you choose not to be a miserable cow." Lauren chuckled at first, but then she started to think about the power she has to *shift* her own mindset and focus on what brings her joy. It may seem silly or simple, but ever since that day, whenever feelings of anger or upset present themselves Lauren repeats that quote to herself and makes a *shift*.

Another way to identify and practice joy is to take a joy inventory. Using a chart template (you can use the one in the Appendix or make your own), write down all the activities that you do most often or most regularly in the left column. Then score that activity on a scale from one to ten, with one representing no joy, five representing a moderate or medium amount of joy, and ten representing the most joyful activity in your life.

This activity can help you in multiple ways. First, it helps you reflect on the activities that you do most and identify which ones bring you the most joy. Depending on how you decide to complete the activity, it can help you reflect honestly on how much joy those activities cultivate. It also helps you think about what activities and experiences you could add to your daily life to increase your joy.

See the Appendix for a blank chart to complete for yourself.

Practice Reminder: "Today I will ..."

Chapter 10
Joy

REFLECT

Here you have an opportunity to take some time and think about joy. You may find it beneficial to write out your responses.

- ❖ This chapter's Elevate quote is directly aligned to joy. Take a moment and read the quote aloud to yourself. See, hear, and feel the words. What resonates with you?
- ❖ When I ask myself, "What brings me joy?" what is the first thing that pops into my head?
  - ➤ What are the second and third things?
- ❖ What can I do right now to cultivate joy in this moment in time?
- ❖ How can I help others to recognize their potential to feel joy?

DISCOVER

If you want to explore this topic further, check out the resources below.

Places:

- The Chopra Center - Created by Deepak Chopra, M.D. - https://chopra.com/

Things:

- "20 Simple Ways to Create Joy Everyday," https://init4thelongrun.com/2018/01/25/create-joy/
- "100 Small Things that Can Bring You Joy," https://www.wisebread.com/100-small-things-that-can-bring-you-joy
- "I Am Light" video - https://www.youtube.com/watch?v=ism8dBjxKvc&fbclid=IwAR0UI8EgdDgqh4ZV5poEIDd0jtF4sS6gmbJm9GrxLzN4NhfG0wMvCN61H3c
- Tarakovsky, M. (2018, July 8). The importance of play for adults. Psych Central. https://psychcentral.com/blog/the-importance-of-play-for-adults#1
- *Work: How to Find Joy and Meaning in Each Hour of The Day* by Thich Nhat Hanh

Chapter 11
Kindness

ELEVATE

I see kindness as a very crucial and important form of self-care. When one is blessed to demonstrate kindness to another person, the act of doing so becomes a blessing to the giver. So, we are blessed to be a blessing to others. When we dig deep in our hearts and truly step out of our comfort zone by choosing to demonstrate kindness in doing something that feels risky to us, for someone with whom we wouldn't normally interact, kindness becomes a form of powerful growth and influence.

—Frances A. Miller, EdD, improvement consultant

PRACTICE

Let's speak kind words! We know the power of our words and the importance of choosing our words carefully (see Chapter 3) regardless of whether those words are spoken, written, or thought. The power of our words ignites tremendous potential for manifestation within our lives. What we think about we bring about all day, every day! When we *give* kindness to others, we *get* kindness back; even if it is not always from the person we gave it to, it boomerangs back in other ways all the time! Let's focus on the energy of kindness as a pathway for all our words. This is so powerful! Let's remember the importance of kindness in our conversations with others and in our own self-talk. Fill in the blank: "I am _____." Keep your words positive and purposeful! We have much more power than we realize.

Here are simple kindness actions that you can do today:

1. Smile and say hello to everyone you encounter.

2. Let someone ahead of you in line or in the car lane.

3. Offer authentic compliments when deemed appropriate.

4. Actively listen to someone else's story or point of view without feeling the need to jump in and tell your story.

5. Offer forgiveness frequently.

6. Relinquish the need to always be right or be the winner.

7. Give someone something.

8. Give yourself or someone else the benefit of the doubt.

Let's change the world … one inter*action* at a time. Kindness really is loaning someone your strength instead of reminding them of their weakness. Dr. Wayne Dyer (2005), in his book *The Power of Intention*, shared that research has shown that a simple act of kindness directed toward another improves the functioning of the immune system and stimulates the production of serotonin in both the recipient of the kindness and in the person extending the kindness. Even more amazing is that people who are observing the act of kindness have similar beneficial results. Imagine this! Kindness extended, received, or observed beneficially impacts the physical health and feelings of everyone involved!

Practice Reminder: "Today I will …"

Chapter 11
Kindness

REFLECT

Here you have an opportunity to take some time and think about kindness. You may find it beneficial to write out your responses.

- ❖ This chapter's Elevate quote is directly aligned to kindness. Take a moment and read the quote aloud to yourself. See, hear, and feel the words. What resonates with you?
- ❖ I will focus my attention on kindness. As I observe the world around me, do I notice different acts of kindness (big or small)?
  - ➢ What did I observe?
- ❖ I will try to do at least three of my own acts of kindness (big or small).
  - ➢ What acts of kindness did I do?
  - ➢ Were they big, small, or both?
  - ➢ How did I feel before, during, and after?
  - ➢ Did I notice any changes or *shifts* in myself?
  - ➢ Did I notice any changes or *shifts* in the other person?
- ❖ Can I take a few moments to remember how it feels when I give or receive an act of kindness?
- ❖ Can I find opportunities to share the importance of kindness with others?

DISCOVER

If you want to explore this topic further, check out the resources below.

Places:

- Random Acts of Kindness Foundation: https://www.randomactsofkindness.org/
- Ripple Kindness Project: https://ripplekindness.org/
- Daily Kindness Digest: https://www.lifevestinside.com/blog/
- Life Vest Inside: https://www.lifevestinside.com/

Things:

- My Simple Acts of Service examples https://www.holyfamily.edu/images/pdfs/service/SimpleActs-Fall2020-editted.pdf
- *The Kindness Boomerang* by Orly Wahba
- Kindness Boomerang—"One Day," https://www.youtube.com/watch?v=nwAYpLVyeFU
- Kirk Franklin—"I Smile" (Video) www.youtube.com/watch?v=Z8SPwT3nQZ8&fbclid=IwAR1jcaEZ5fs7ERZEVzWKEN0iSlJNeuhwlC42voXSdZl35xocJ2A4JZeYvS0

Chapter 12
Love and Fear

ELEVATE

THE BEST WAY to bring love and prosperity into your life is to bless everything and give thanks for every increase which comes your way as a gift from God. As you learn to bless and give thanks for everything, you are actually putting into practice one of the great laws of prosperity and plenty, for with love and blessings comes increase.
—Eileen Caddy, spiritual leader

PRACTICE

Several years ago, Gerry learned a powerful lesson and it changed the way she looks at every person, situation, and event. Gerry carries this lesson with her every day. There are only two pure emotions – love and fear. Every **f**eeling, **e**motion, **a**ction, and **t**hought (FEAT) fall into one of two categories. It is either in the category of love or in the category of fear. We can typically identify love because it is positive and feels good. Fear is harder. When we are feeling anxious, frustrated, jealous, lonely, petty, angry, etc. we are actually in a space of fear. All those feelings fall into the fear category. This is the biggest lesson of all: *choose love!* Fear is anything that is not love.

We can test this out with any FEAT we might have. Let's give it a try. Right now, create a T-chart. Gerry likes T-charts because they are a graphic organizer in which you can examine two facets of any topic. On the T-chart, put the word "Love" on one side and "Fear" on the other. Think about love first, as that is much more fun! Take a moment and list all of the FEATs that show up in your life as love. Gerry wrote down smiles, hugs, joyful, laughter, patience, and kindness. Next, think of FEATs that don't feel loving, but might not feel fear-based. Think of experiences you may have had in traffic, in your classroom, at the grocery store, in your home, at a social gathering, or even while alone. Think of those times when, in your gut, you did not feel love. Write these words in the "Fear" column. Gerry wrote down agitated, gossiping, sarcastic, judgmental, and rage.

Love is the most powerful tool everyone has to best navigate this world. When we live in the column of love, the possibilities are endless. From this day forward, try to watch your FEATs with a laser focus. When you find yourself thinking a thought or displaying an action that is not in the "Love" column, this is your instant opportunity to shift your thinking. This shifting strategy works with big and small challenges equally. The moment you feel that non-loving feeling, you can identify it and choose to shift your thinking. Getting agitated or angry will not change the situation, and could possibly have a negative impact on more people than we can imagine. We can observe the FEATs of those around us. Every person who comes to us in an attacking, rude, or angry fashion is coming from a place of fear. When we encounter these types of interactions, we can quickly shift how we choose to respond. Once you are aware of the love and fear strategy, there is no turning back.

Practice Reminder: "Today I will …"

Chapter 12
Love and Fear

REFLECT

Here you have an opportunity to take some time and think about love and fear. You may find it beneficial to write out your responses.

- ❖ This chapter's Elevate quote is directly aligned to love and fear. Take a moment and read the quote aloud to yourself. See, hear, and feel the words. What resonates with you?
- ❖ Have I ever felt angry, frustrated, jealous, disappointed, or disturbed?
  - ➢ Do I sometimes feel justified to hold on to those feelings?
- ❖ When I encounter feelings that fall into the "Fear" column, what can I do?
- ❖ I will take notice of conversations I have or events that are occurring around me that are steeped in a fear-based stance. Can I recognize the fear?
  - ➢ Can I flip the switch to love?
- ❖ Can I find opportunities to share with others about the importance of choosing love over fear?

DISCOVER

If you want to explore this topic further, check out the resources below.

People:

- Marianne Williamson, internationally acclaimed author and lecturer
  www.marianne.com
- Lisa Natoli
  https://lisanatoli.com/40day
- Gabrielle Bernstein, author & self-described spirit junkie
  https://gabbybernstein.com/about/meet-gabby
- Laura Bushnell
  https://laurabushnell.com/about/

Places:

- "Shifting From Fear to Love" course, https://www.dailyom.com/cgi-bin/courses/courseoverview.cgi?cid=240

Things:

- *Return to Love* by Marianne Williamson
- *Shifting From Fear to Love* by Gabrielle Bernstein
- *Life Magic* by Laura Bushnell
  The Gift by Laura Bushnell
  You Are a Rose by Laura Bushnell
  https://laurabushnell.com/shop/

Chapter 13
Music

ELEVATE

*With so much division in the world today, performing and listening to music
is a wonderful tool to experience different cultures and learn about each other
so that we may better understand each other to live in harmony.*
—Rick Hood, music teacher

PRACTICE

Music truly touches the soul. When we hear a song that's connected to a memory, we are immediately transported to that time and space. We can feel the emotions, smell the fragrances, feel the temperature, and even feel our body change by getting warmer or cooler. You may remember the song that was playing during your first kiss. You may remember a particular song from a concert or movie. You may remember a song that made you laugh or cry. There are many layers attached to the music of our lives. We also tend to favor some types of music over others. You may love country music but don't care for opera. You may connect with sing-along songs, or you may prefer soothing instrumental music. You may have a genre of music you listen to for studying and another genre of music for cleaning the house. You may enjoy classical or music from your youth, or you may like to connect with new cutting-edge music. Our musical go-tos are unique to each person. When we know which types of music rev us up, slow us down, make us happy, or turn us to tears, we can use music as a purposeful self-care strategy. Gerry has recently found that listening to new music and new artists opens her creativity and problem-solving processes. Gerry is not quite sure why, but she would venture to guess that since it's new to her she can't sing or hum along, but she's paying attention to the words and sounds and keeping her mind and soul open to new possibilities. Tried and true music and lyrics are like an old and comfortable pair of jeans. They fit perfectly and take us to a place, space, or time of good memories; they have been comfortably worn thin in all the right places to match us perfectly.

Using music as a self-care strategy is very personal and individual. Research has shown that if we are looking to address stress, selecting slow-paced or classical music is a good selection.

Practice Reminder: "Today I will …"

Chapter 13
Music

REFLECT

Here you have an opportunity to take some time and think about music. You may find it beneficial to write out your responses.

- ❖ This chapter's Elevate quote is directly aligned to music. Take a moment and read the quote aloud to yourself. See, hear, and feel the words. What resonates with you?
- ❖ What genre of music or specific song(s) makes me smile? Cry? Get motivated? Feel calm?
- ❖ What songs would be on the soundtrack of my life? Why?
  - ➢ What feelings, thoughts, or memories do these songs bring about?
- ❖ What songs would I add to a playlist dedicated to when I am exercising, or when I need to be productive and focus, or when I want to relax, or when I need an emotional release, etc.?
- ❖ Can I see this practice being helpful in my classroom?
  - ➢ How can I use music with my students at specific times during the day?
- ❖ Can I find opportunities to share the importance of music with others?

DISCOVER

If you want to explore this topic further, check out the resources below.

Places:

- Self-care music playlists: https://www.urmc.rochester.edu/MediaLibraries/URMCMedia/Eastman%20Performance%20Medicine/documents/Self-Care-Music-Playlist.pdf

Things:

- "Stop. Pause. Play—Using Music for Self-Care," https://www.tendacademy.ca/using-music-self-care/
- "Using Music for Stress Reduction and Self-Care," https://www.crestbd.ca/2020/04/09/music-self-care/
- "Using Music for Self-Care," https://content.westmusic.com/using-music-for-self-care/
- "How to Incorporate Music Therapy into Your Self-Care Routine," https://www.trueself.com/how-to-incorporate-music-therapy-into-your-self-care-routine-2645609521.html
- "Music Therapy," https://www.stress.org/education/music-therapy
- "3 Simple Ways to Use Music as Part of Your Self-Care Plan," https://www.liveconnectedny.com/single-post/2016/06/21/3-simple-ways-to-use-music-as-part-of-your-selfcare-plan

Chapter 14
Nutrition

ELEVATE

Your relationship with food is always reflecting back to you, your relationship with yourself. I've never met a person who truly loved and respected themselves who had a disordered relationship with food. Once you can learn to eat like you love yourself, school is out.
—Linda Leland, coach and women's global influencer

Adding our love to every recipe we make enhances and transcends its nutritional value into magical nourishment for our souls and our bodies. With every bite, it reminds us that we are worthy of receiving love, and this awareness brings joy!
—Diana Silva, founder of Molé Mama

PRACTICE

"We have the best, most perfect diet just for you." That promise has been made many times. Nutrition, or lack thereof, has a profound effect on a person's body and mind. Lauren is a self-proclaimed emotional eater. Lauren makes the excuse to eat junk when she is happy and wants to celebrate, when she is sad, or when she feels defeated. This emotional eating never makes her feel any better, so why does Lauren do it? As a school counselor, Lauren is always trying to practice what she preaches to her coworkers, students, and families. Eating a balanced, healthy diet is a key element to staying physically, mentally, and emotionally healthy. We all know that food can be a form of comfort in trying times. We don't want to take that away, but we also know that too much junk and processed food can lead to much worse problems. Here's the answer: there is no one-size-fits-all diet (or anything)! This is tied to love and fear (see Chapter 12). Each one of us is different. Get to know yourself, connect with what feels right, eliminate guilt, and follow that path. Consult with experts and medical practitioners whom you trust, who know you, and who have your best interests at heart.

All of the other chapters are designed to help and encourage you to increase your attention and awareness, *shift* your thinking and perspective, and give you strategies to practice when your inner flame feels low. To bring more awareness to your nutrition, try to write down everything you eat during one day of your choosing. Commit to the day in the morning when you wake. Say to yourself, "I am going to write down everything I eat and drink today, no judgment!" This doesn't have to be fancy; it can be just a list. At the end of the day, spend some time with that list and reflect on the nutrition choices you made. Is there anything that you can eliminate? Is there anything you can monitor to ensure you are consuming in moderation? Is there anything you can add to improve your diet? Follow your own personal path. You know what to do!

Practice Reminder: "Today I will …"

Chapter 14
Nutrition

REFLECT

Here you have an opportunity to take some time and think about nutrition. You may find it beneficial to write out your responses.

- ❖ This chapter's Elevate quote is directly aligned to nutrition. Take a moment and read the quote aloud to yourself. See, hear, and feel the words. What resonates with you?
- ❖ Did I adjust any of my food choices because I committed to journaling my food choices?
- ❖ After reviewing my food choices, was there anything I would have done differently?
- ❖ How do I feel about my nutrition? Do I think it has an impact on my overall well-being?
- ❖ Try identifying one unhealthy choice and replacing it with a healthy choice. Do I feel any different?
- ❖ Can I find opportunities to share the importance of nutrition with others?

DISCOVER

If you want to explore this topic further, check out the resources below.

People:

- Diana Silva, Molé Mama
  - o Book: *Molé Mama: A Memoir of Love, Cooking, and Loss*
  - o Website: https://www.molemama.com/
  - o Podcast: https://www.molemama.com/mole-mama-cooking-with-love-podcast
  - o Videos: https://www.molemama.com/all-cooking-videos
- Dr. Christiane Northrup, MD
  https://www.drnorthrup.com/
- Jon Gabriel, author and creator of The Gabriel Method: A Mind-Body Approach to Permanent, Sustainable Weight Loss: https://www.thegabrielmethod.com/

Places:

- AndThenSheShines.com
  - o Signature programs: Food Rules, Diets and Love (5 Week Intensive Course)
  - o Eat Like You Love Yourself Academy (Group coaching platform), Unconditional Self Love and Cooking with Joy and Simplicity
  - o 10-Day Reset Cleanse
- Dietary Guidelines for Americans: https://www.fns.usda.gov/cnpp/dietary-guidelines-americans Things: "The Critical Role Nutrition Plays in Mental Health," https://psychcentral.com/blog/the-critical-role-nutrition-plays-in-mental-health/
- "A Nutritional Psychiatrist On How To *Actually* Enjoy Healthy Eating," https://www.mindbodygreen.com/articles/how-to-enjoy-healthy-eating-from-nutritional-psychiatrist?utm_source=facebook.com&utm_medium=social&utm_campaign=facebook--1-6-2021&utm_term=food&utm_content=new&fbclid=IwAR0QZMSQNHjotu6TjM1RaSHCdsy3uTNHJA1UFvQnMz2JHIseDrg4WK9PMe0
- *Women's Wisdom Women's Bodies* by Dr. Christiane Northrup, MD
- Naidoo, U. (2018). *Gut feelings: How food affects your mood.* https://www.health.harvard.edu/blog/gut-feelings-how-food-affects-your-mood-2018120715548
- "8 steps to mindful eating," https://www.health.harvard.edu/staying-healthy/8-steps-to-mindful-eating

Chapter 15
Out Loud Laughter

ELEVATE

If at the end of the day, you haven't laughed; you haven't lived!
—Christine Borelli, educational leader

PRACTICE

Laughter is amazingly good for your health. The Mayo Clinic (2019) shared that laughter relaxes the whole body, boosts the immune system, stimulates organs, soothes tension, relieves pain, and improves your mood. These short- and long-term effects trigger the release of endorphins, protect the heart, burn calories, and may even help you live longer.

Gerry loves to laugh. If you know her, you know that she loves to laugh, and she has a very unique and contagious laugh. These two characteristics have been with Gerry her entire life. When Gerry meets old friends from her grade-school years, they also remember her laughter. Years ago, Gerry hosted a Saint Patrick's Day party at her home. Everyone was having a great time. Gerry's friend's husband is a character, and at parties, he is the resident comedian. Well, he was telling jokes and stories, and everyone was laughing. Someone came up to Gerry and shared that they hadn't had a belly laugh like that in years. Gerry was wowed by this because she laughs like that at least once a day.

Gerry has many tried and true classroom stories that she can remember at a moment's notice to bring about a belly laugh. Years ago, during Gerry's first few years of teaching, a student walked into the third-grade classroom wearing a T-shirt with a large sun on it. Inside the sun were the words, "A day without sex is like a day without sunshine." When Gerry read the student's shirt, she had to control her laughter. Gerry asked him where he got his shirt, and he mentioned that it was from home and he had just put it on. Gerry got him a new shirt to wear. Thirty years later, when Gerry thinks of this scenario, she laughs out loud. Joyful celebratory laughter is a quick and easy way to raise our vibrational level. Below are some ways to *shift* into a space for laughter.

- Tune in to or sign up for the comedy channel on your television or radio station.
- Think about what old TV shows or movies made you laugh out loud when you were a kid and go back and watch them.
- Join a Facebook group that focuses on positivity and laughter.
- Find memes that make you laugh and post them where you will see them frequently.
- Save links from YouTube or other sites with funny videos that you can go back to when you need a boost.
- Think about a current or former student who made you laugh, drew a funny picture, or wrote a funny sentence or story. Save that memory or actual piece of work to look back on when you need to.

Practice Reminder: "Today I will …"

Chapter 15
Out Loud Laughter

REFLECT

Here you have an opportunity to take some time and think about out loud laughter. You may find it beneficial to write out your responses.

- ❖ This chapter's Elevate quote is directly aligned to out loud laughter. Take a moment and read the quote aloud to yourself. See, hear, and feel the words. What resonates with you?
- ❖ When was the last time I had a belly laugh or when I laughed so hard that my cheeks hurt?
- ❖ Which strategy above might help me *shift* into a state of laughter when I need to?
- ❖ Take some time to think about or write down memories that make you laugh.
- ❖ Can I find opportunities to share the importance of laughter with others?

DISCOVER

If you want to explore this topic further, check out the resources below.

Places:

- LOL!: https://laughoutloud.com/

Things:

- "Laughter is the Best Medicine," https://www.helpguide.org/articles/mental-health/laughter-is-the-best-medicine.htm#:~:text=Endorphins%20promote%20an%20overall%20sense,attack%20and%20other%20cardiovascular%20problems.
- Mayo Clinic Staff (2019) *Stress relief from laughter? It's not a joke.* https://www.mayoclinic.org/healthy-lifestyle/stress-management/in-depth/stress-relief/art-20044456
- Doskock, P. (2016). Happily ever laughter. *Psychology Today.* https://www.psychologytoday.com/us/articles/199607/happily-ever-laughter
- "The Healing Power Of Laughter: Ways To Use Humor As Part Of Self Care", https://www.wellsanfrancisco.com/laughter-humor-self-care/

Chapter 16
Prayer

ELEVATE

Each morning in that tender time between dark and dawn, I give myself ten to fifteen minutes to "connect" to that which sustains me. In my life, this is God… in your life, it might be something different. For some, it is peace, love, beauty, truth, a general sense of something larger that is—the force or source of all things. It really does not matter. What matters is making the connection.

I liken this to plugging in a lamp in a dark room. Once plugged in—the light receives the energy it needs to light up the room. The "plugging in" makes the light possible. Once on—the lamp illuminates the space, making it easier to navigate without getting lost or tripping over things. Plugged into Source at the start of each day provides the same function. If I plug in, I don't get lost in the stressors or overwhelm of the day and I find that it is much easier to navigate through the tricky terrain of all of the things I might face that day.

The act of "plugging in" might take shape as a prayer or recitation of a mantra or affirmation. For me, "plugging in" at the start of each day means that I rest quietly and I envision myself surrounded by the light of the Divine. The experience that accompanies this ten-minute "plug in" is akin to being held in a strong, protective, benevolent energy that I then carry with me into my day. Lit from within, I am better able to be a beacon of hope, wisdom, inspiration, strength and compassion for anyone I encounter. This "plugging in" practice has been with me for many years. It is simple, effective and so valuable.

—Christine Kiesinger, PhD, professor

PRACTICE

Prayer is a support system. Some people participate in a formal prayer practice. Some people lean into prayer when something serious occurs in their lives. Some people would say that they don't pray, and maybe that is because the word "prayer" is so closely associated with religion. Many people separate prayer from meditation. Gerry looks at this as a forever circle. In prayer, Gerry places her question, request, point of concern, or fear. Then the second half of the circle is meditation; it's the time when the answers often surface. As Dr. Kiesinger stated above, they connect to what sustains them, which in their life is God. Maybe that aligns with your beliefs or maybe not. We can all practice "plugging in" to what sustains us. Try to think about what or who that might be for you—God(s), formal religion, nature, ancestors, music, art, family, etc. For our practice, we are offering an opportunity to reflect upon what we believe or what we might like to explore further. Let's *shift* all of our perceptions from worries, complaints, aggravations, and annoyances to the direction of what sustains us and keeps our inner candle burning brightly. In a snap we can change our perspective, our current moment, our day, and our life.

Practice Reminder: "Today I will …"

Chapter 16
Prayer

REFLECT

Here you have an opportunity to take some time and think about prayer. You may find it beneficial to write out your responses.

- ❖ This chapter's Elevate quote is directly aligned to prayer. Take a moment and read the quote aloud to yourself. See, hear, and feel the words. What resonates with you?
- ❖ What are my beliefs?
- ❖ What parts of the "Elevate" and "Practice" sections resonated with me?
- ❖ Am I open to learning about others' beliefs?
- ❖ What sustains me?
- ❖ How will I attempt to "plug in"?
- ❖ Can I find opportunities to share the importance of prayer with others?

DISCOVER

If you want to explore this topic further, check out the resources below.

Places:

- • Harvard Divinity School - Prayers for Peace and Justice https://hds.harvard.edu/life-at-hds/religious-and-spiritual-life/peace-and-justice/prayers-for-peace-and-justice
- • Teachers of God Foundation - https://www.teachersofgod.org/
- • Center for Action & Contemplation: https://cac.org

Things:

- • *The Interfaith Prayer Book* by Ted Brownstein
- • *God Calling* edited by A.J. Russell: https://www.johnhuntpublishing.com/circle-books/authors/a-j-russell

Chapter 17
Quit

ELEVATE

Knowing when to move ahead or to move on, is focusing on the opportunities of "tomorrow" and not dwelling on your "yesterdays." Being a lifelong learner is realizing that every day and every experience becomes a new opportunity for growth and expansion, you're never quitting you're just always beginning something new.
—Dayna Gibbs-Bowser, MEd, educator

PRACTICE

Quitting often has a negative connotation. We typically don't want to identify ourselves as being a quitter. As educators, we are encouraged to never give up and we encourage others to do the same. Saying "no" or quitting is hard, but not saying "no" can make you feel exhausted, stressed, and irritable. Difficulty saying "no" and accepting too many tasks, roles, or jobs might be undermining your efforts to improve your quality of life. Taking on too much may negatively impact your quality time with your family or friends (Collingwood, 2016). Think of what no longer serves you and can be removed. There are 24 hours or 1,440 minutes in each day. After sleeping a minimum of 7 hours (420 minutes), you have 17 hours (1,020 minutes) to be authentically engaged with life.

These two practices can help you reflect on and identify what you may be able to quit. The first practice is simple. Have you ever heard someone say, "I have to take something off my plate"? Educators pile on important objects, people, projects, challenges, and initiatives on their plates and never remove anything. Using a paper plate and art supplies, create a collage of everything that is on your plate of life. Honor and congratulate yourself for all that you do! Now, what can or should be removed? Take those things off your plate literally and figuratively! You may want to remove some concrete items such as belonging to organizations, volunteering, household chores, etc. You may want to remove some thoughts and beliefs such as perfectionism, resentment, or people-pleasing. The choice is yours. You are important. Your work is powerful and very much needed.

The second practice is creating a Thank You and Goodbye Box (TYG Box). Find a box; the box you choose to use is completely up to you. The strategy is to think about some internal and external experiences that are currently in your life but no longer serve you, your purpose, or your higher good. This is a highly personalized strategy and being honest with yourself is critical. Write what you want to quit on a slip of paper. Place your words in your box. Take time to sit quietly and think about what you are quitting. Connect with the excitement and confidence you have in eliminating these experiences from your present moment and beyond. You can peek into this box regularly to make sure you are honoring your promise to yourself. You may add more words at any time. Celebrate every one of the 1,020 minutes gifted to you each day!

Practice Reminder: "Today I will …"

Chapter 17
Quit

REFLECT

Here you have an opportunity to take some time and think about the need to possibly quit some things. You may find it beneficial to write out your responses.

- ❖ This chapter's Elevate quote is directly aligned to the need to possibly quit some things. Take a moment and read the quote aloud to yourself. See, hear, and feel the words. What resonates with you?
- ❖ How do I feel now that I have identified some experiences to quit? Do I see myself following through?
  - ➢ If following through is a barrier, can I take smaller steps toward quitting?
- ❖ What new beginnings, happenings, and experiences would I like to call into my life?
- ❖ Can I find opportunities to share with others about the importance of quitting what no longer serves us?

DISCOVER

If you want to explore this topic further, check out the resources below.

People:

- Elizabeth Lindsay - Angel With An Edge
  - o Angel With An Edge radio show - https://angelwithanedge.com/radio-show/
  - o Blog - https://angelwithanedge.com/category/blog/
  - o Website - www.angelwithanedge.com

Places:

- Positively Positive: https://www.positivelypositive.com
  - o Blogs and broadcasts from contributors and thought leaders in positivity such as Gretchen Rubin (The Happiness Project), Christina Rasmussen (Second Firsts: Live, Laugh, and Love Again), and life coach Terri Cole
- THE MISSION - https://medium.com/the-mission

Things:

- "How to Let Go of What No Longer Serves You," https://medium.com/the-mission/this-is-how-to-let-go-of-what-no-longer-serves-you-so-you-can-attract-more-of-what-you-really-need-1a01259c8dea
- Vozza, S. (2016) *The ultimate guide to saying no to things you don't want to do.* https://www.fastcompany.com/3056562/the-ultimate-guide-to-saying-no-to-things-you-dont-want-to
- Collingwood, J. (2016). Learning to say no [webpage]. Retrieved from: https://psychcentral.com/lib/learning-to-say-no#1

Chapter 18
Reading

ELEVATE

To read is to embark on a journey … to learn the main claims of a text, to explore the unknown or unfamiliar, to read between the lines … We stand at the crossroads between the text and ourselves, ready to make sense of the signs, to make connections, to fill in the gaps with our own wonderings. Inquiring minds purchase passage to the most mysterious of places - the world of another.
—Patty Cruice, EdD, educational consultant, author, and retired principal

PRACTICE

Reading is both a legal and socially acceptable way to escape reality. When the light of our candle feels or seems dim, we can take a mini vacation into another's story, an interesting topic or current event, or a hobby. As educators, we all know the importance of the written word. We learn new information, we solidify what we know to be true, and we are challenged to create questions and points of inquiry based on what we have read and what we have learned. As we have shared earlier, there are a finite number of minutes in each day, and we have to be intentional and purposeful in how we use them. Many educators save their fun reading and their personal reading for the summer months. That's typically only two months. The practice here is to find a way to incorporate personal daily reading into your everyday experience. Take a few moments to think about areas of current (and possibly future) interest for you. You might want to read more about spirituality, sewing, politics, or cooking. You might want to have time to read more love stories or biographies. Think about what brings you joy and go with that. In Chapter 17, we encouraged you to permanently take things off of your plate. If you read for ten minutes every day because that's literally all the time you can squeeze out, you will finish that book and then be able to move on to the next one.

Practice Reminder: "Today I will …"

Chapter 18
Reading

REFLECT

Here you have an opportunity to take some time and think about reading. You may find it beneficial to write out your responses.

- ❖ This chapter's Elevate quote is directly aligned to reading. Take a moment and read the quote aloud to yourself. See, hear, and feel the words. What resonates with you?
- ❖ Do I feel that finding time for reading is important to me or helpful for me?
- ❖ What do I like to read?
- ❖ What genres get me excited or interested?
- ❖ If reading is important to me and helpful for me, how can I find time to include reading in my day or week?
- ❖ Can I find opportunities to share the importance of finding the time to read with others?

DISCOVER

If you want to explore this topic further, check out the resources below.

Places:

- Open Library - https://openlibrary.org/
- World Cat - https://www.worldcat.org/
- Many Books - https://manybooks.net/
- Audible - https://www.audible.com/ (30-day free trial, requires a fee after 1ˢᵗ month)
- Awakin.org: https://www.awakin.org/read/ - weekly recommended reading to encourage and facilitate insight and reflection
- Check out your local county library *and* your school's or district's libraries

Things:

- *Gift From the Sea* by Anne Morrow Lindbergh
- "7 Reasons Why Reading is the Best Self Care," https://www.goodnet.org/articles/7-reasons-reading-best-self-care
- Parker J. Palmer, "ON the BRINK of EVERYTHING," https://onthebrinkofeverything.com/

Chapter 19
Sleep

ELEVATE

As a teacher, (thank you for recognizing daycare as teaching) the single most important thing I can do to prepare each day is get a good night's sleep. These angels and their growing brains have been entrusted to my care. I have to be physically, mentally and psychologically ready to fulfill that trust. All the prep work and lesson planning is meaningless if I am physically ill prepared by being sleep deprived. You can't let the little darlings catch ya nappin'!
—Marybeth Granville Neroni, child care teacher

PRACTICE

Think about a time when you woke up from a good night's sleep and felt energized and refreshed. You felt like a million bucks! Although we know what that feels like, many educators cannot claim this as part of their regular routine. Did you know that "teacher's reported having poor mental health for 11 or more days per month at twice the rate of the general US workforce. They also reported lower-than-recommended levels of health outcomes and sleep per night?" (Educator Quality of Life Survey, 2017, p. i).

It is a happy coincidence that sleep comes later in this book because the earlier strategies can address many of the things that get in the way of your sleep. Negativity, pressure at school, a never-ending to-do list, and lack of time can linger on an educator's mind and cause disruptions in their sleep. As you read through previous and future chapters (breathe, hope, music, reading, yoga, exercise, and more), you can use these strategies to help with sleep. For example, the practices of taking deep breaths to handle frustration or anxiety in your classroom, finding hope in a stressful situation at school, or spreading kindness to encourage your students to spread kindness to each other, or whatever you decided to do may inadvertently help you get a longer, more restful night of sleep. It is like a domino effect.

The strategies and practices featured in this book take practice and are a work in progress, so instant gratification or immediate results may not happen. You can take some steps to focus on getting a longer, more restful night of sleep. Here are a few small steps you can take: turn technology off thirty minutes before bedtime, avoid napping later in the day, create a bedtime routine for yourself, exercise on a regular basis, limit caffeine and large meals late in the day, and adjust the temperature or lighting to invite relaxation (National Institute on Aging n.d.). A colleague once shared with Lauren that they keep a notebook on their nightstand which they use to write down any thoughts, ideas, worries, or to-do's if they are having trouble falling asleep or if they wake up in the middle of the night. This could help take those things off your mind and let you get back to your restful night's sleep.

Practice Reminder: "Today I will …"

Chapter 19
Sleep

REFLECT

Here you have an opportunity to take some time and think about sleep. You may find it beneficial to write out your responses.

- ❖ This chapter's Elevate quote is directly aligned to sleep. Take a moment and read the quote aloud to yourself. See, hear, and feel the words. What resonates with you?
- ❖ Is sleep an issue for me? If so, do I have trouble falling asleep, staying asleep, or both?
- ❖ Think about the last week or two. Estimate how many times my sleep was restful and refreshing.
- ❖ If I have issues with sleep or want to get more sleep, how can I take steps to do that?
  - ➢ What barriers are in my way?
  - ➢ What steps would I take?
- ❖ Go back to the chapter on breath (Chapter 2) and check out some of the resources there that might assist with sleep.
- ❖ Can I find opportunities to share the importance of quality sleep with others?

DISCOVER

If you want to explore this topic further, check out the resources below.

Places:

- Lifewire - 5 Websites That Can Help You Sleep Better: https://www.lifewire.com/websites-can-help-you-sleep-better-4015323
- American Academy of Sleep Medicine: https://aasm.org
- World Sleep Day: https://worldsleepday.org/toolkit
- Sleep Foundation: https://www.sleepfoundation.org
- Dr. Rubin Naiman, PhD, Transforming Sleep & Dreams: https://drnaiman.com

Things:

- Sleep Foundation - Healthy Sleep Tips: https://www.sleepfoundation.org/articles/healthy-sleep-tips
- "How to Sleep Better," https://www.helpguide.org/articles/sleep/getting-better-sleep.htm
- "6 steps to sleep better," https://www.mayoclinic.org/healthy-lifestyle/adult-health/in-depth/sleep/art-20048379
- "How Sleep and Nature Enhance Your Thinking," https://www.psychologytoday.com/us/blog/the-modern-brain/202009/how-sleep-and-nature-enhance-your-thinking?fbclid=IwAR0Dl7UfdSK8JRFGKTfBbtxU1pVx_yALM-k-RaTAXOJL6CwUrCY9OU1jZtg
- Drake C; Roehrs T; Shambroom J; Roth T. Caffeine effects on sleep taken 0, 3, or 6 hours before going to bed. *J Clin Sleep Med* 2013;9(11):1195-1200. https://www.ncbi.nlm.nih.gov/pmc/articles/PMC3805807/
- Smith, M., Robinson, L., & Segal, J. (2018). How to sleep better: Simple steps to getting a good night's sleep. *HelpGuide*.
  https://www.helpguide.org/articles/sleep/getting-better-sleep.htm

Chapter 20
Thoughts

ELEVATE

The LIGHT in you is TOO BRIGHT to fail.
—Corinne Zupko, EdDS, award-winning author of *From Anxiety to Love*

PRACTICE

Thoughts are pure vibrational energy. All thoughts have unbelievable power. What we think about becomes our reality. Let's be very, very, very intentional regarding what thoughts we allow to fill our mind! If a negative, jealous, angry, or fearful thought pops up (and it will), let's recognize it. Then, send it on its way and replace it with a loving thought! We know the difference between a loving thought and the other kind by how we feel while having that thought. Check in with your body. How does that feel in your head, your gut, and your shoulders? We know!

Let's look at the word "imagine." What do you see? Do you see "I'm a genie" (phonetically)? We all have "genie-like" qualities to create our lives exactly as we want them to be. We can't do this for others (although we often wish we could). It's an inside job! Let's think about and journal about what we imagine for our future. Release the restrictions of feeling too old, young, tall, short, rich, or poor. *Shift* your thoughts to the positive. Let's be specific and clear. Gerry has personally found that when she immerses herself in this practice and sits in love (not fear), the enchantment (so to speak) surfaces. Imagine the possibilities!

Our thoughts create our life. Are we paying attention to what we are thinking about? When we work with students at school, we often talk about the impact of thoughts and self-talk. We try to point out how negative thoughts or self-talk make them feel compared to positive thoughts or self-talk. What we think about really does impact our life. We encourage you to check in with yourself throughout each day and make sure that your thoughts are aligned with what you want to believe about yourself and your life.

Practice Reminder: "Today I will …"

Chapter 20
Thoughts

REFLECT

Here you have an opportunity to take some time and think about thoughts. You may find it beneficial to write out your responses.

- ❖ This chapter's Elevate quote is directly aligned to your thoughts. Take a moment and read the quote aloud to yourself. See, hear, and feel the words. What resonates with you?
- ❖ Am I paying attention to what I am thinking about?
- ❖ Am I willing to *shift* my thinking when I realize I am having a negative thought?
- ❖ Can I accept the belief that my thoughts create my life?
- ❖ Will I accept the positive thoughts that I change from negative thoughts?
- ❖ Can I find opportunities to share the importance of our thoughts with others?

DISCOVER

If you want to explore this topic further, check out the resources below.

Things:

- From Anxiety To Love: A Radical New Approach for Letting Go of Fear and Finding Lasting Peace (New World Library, 2018).https://FromAnxietyToLove.com
- Books by Florence Scovel Shinn:
  - o *The Game of Life and How to Play It*
  - o *Your Word Is Your Wand*
  - o *The Secret Door to Success*
  - o *Collection of Florence's works* (4 complete books)
- Growth Mindset - https://www.mindsetworks.com/science/
- "The Power of Believing You Can Improve," https://www.ted.com/speakers/carol_dweck
- Fredrickson, B.L. 2013. "Positive Emotions Broaden and Build." In *Advances in Experimental Social Psychology, Vol. 47,* ed. https://www.sciencedirect.com/science/article/pii/B9780124072367000012
- "The Power of Positive Self-Talk," https://www.psychologytoday.com/us/blog/hope-relationships/201605/the-power-positive-self-talk

Chapter 21
CommUnity

ELEVATE

As teachers, we are role models who possess the knowledge, the training, and the desire to unite people, especially at the toughest times imaginable. We collaborate with our colleagues, students, their parents, and the greater community through our focus on the future, and by our ongoing demonstration of the skills necessary for flexibility and resilience. We do all of this through our confidence, commitment, and dedication to our students and the profession.
—Dr. Jeanne Dagna, educational consultant

PRACTICE

"Humans are, after all, inherently social beings. When people are asked what pleasures contribute most to happiness, the overwhelming majority rate love, intimacy, and social affiliation above wealth or fame, even above physical health" (Cacioppo, J. T. and Patrick, W. 2008). Unity is the state of being united or joined as a whole. It is important to be connected with a group or groups of like-minded people. Being connected, being united, and having a tribe creates a level of combined energy and problem-solving that is magical. There are two key pieces to building your tribe: shared interest and a platform for communicating.

For thousands and thousands of years, people all over the world have used circles to unite. People have used circles to share stories, solve problems, discuss important topics, and more. Our ancestors have modeled how to use a circle to create and maintain unity within the community. As time has passed, we have become more individualistic in our thinking and actions, causing us to move away (intentionally or unintentionally) from the circle. Practice or encourage unity by intentionally starting a new circle by linking people together, whether in your personal or professional life. Be open and willing to listen to others, and glean the truth from each one. A circle, like a wheel, has many spokes which lead to the hub or center. Every spoke is necessary to make that wheel strong and well-balanced; never try to take one away. Accept that each spoke, or person in the circle, is necessary and is a part of the whole. With the hub in mind, unite in the things you can unite in and ignore the things which cause division. Reflect on your circle often to ensure that your circle is strong.

Practice Reminder: "Today I will …"

Chapter 21
CommUnity

REFLECT

Here you have an opportunity to take some time and think about community. You may find it beneficial to write out your responses.

- ❖ This chapter's Elevate quote is directly aligned to community. Take a moment and read the quote aloud to yourself. See, hear, and feel the words. What resonates with you?
- ❖ Visualize, list, or identify the current members of my circle(s).
  - ➤ Do I use my circle to celebrate the positive moments in life?
  - ➤ Is there anyone who needs to be removed from my circle(s)?
  - ➤ Am I intentionally showing up in my circle to be there for others when they need me?
  - ➤ How can I strengthen the links and bonds in my life?
- ❖ Do I find myself without a circle or do I feel that I don't "truly belong" in any circle(s)?
  - ➤ Identify one person to create a bond with in any area of my life.
  - ➤ Reflect on potential gaps in my life to identify where new circles could grow.
  - ➤ Consider joining a professional, religious, political, social, academic, spiritual, or special-interest group either in-person or virtually.
- ❖ Can I find opportunities to share the importance of intentionally connecting with others?

DISCOVER

If you want to explore this topic further, check out the resources below.

Places:

- The Circle Way: A Leader in Every Chair - http://www.thecircleway.net
- Volunteer Match: Organization to assist with locating volunteer opportunities, https://www.volunteermatch.org

Things:

- "How to Build a Circle of Friends That Will Lift You Higher," https://www.psychreg.org/circle-of-friends/
- "Building and Keeping a Circle of Friends," https://psychcentral.com/lib/building-and-keeping-a-circle-of-friends/
- "Four Ways To Find Your Soul Circle," https://www.vanpraagh.com/four-ways-to-find-your-soul-circle/
- Cacioppo, J. T. & Patrick, W. (2008) *Loneliness: Human nature and the need for social connection.* New York: Norton,.https://www.wsj.com/articles/SB122773240294660733

Chapter 22
Voice

ELEVATE

> Speak to yourself like you're someone you truly love.
> —Linda Elliott, intuitive healer, certified reiki master
> and teacher, channeler of our sun's energy

PRACTICE

Your voice is both the sound produced and the attitude expressed; it is your individual, authentic voice. As educators, we need both of those to work well together to instruct and inspire our students. We use the combination of sounds produced to transfer information and tell stories, but we also need the attitude behind the sounds to provide the inspiration, connection, and meaning. We use our voice to teach. Our voice is a tool; one that we use every day. Sometimes we take our voice for granted and view it just as a tool for teaching. Or maybe we sometimes don't take care of our whole voice, both the physical aspects (the sounds produced) and the emotional, social, and communicative aspects (the attitude expressed). How do you take care of the physical aspects of your voice? Maybe you rest your voice or drink tea with lemon. How do you take care of the emotional, social, and communicative aspects of your voice? Maybe you bounce an idea off of a trusted colleague or friend, or you practice being assertive in front of your bedroom mirror before an important meeting.

We may not realize the power of our voice. Have you ever found yourself in a situation where you wanted to say something but you didn't? Have you ever found yourself in a situation where you knew what you wanted to say but you weren't sure how to say it? Many of us have experienced this hesitation or insecurity. When we don't speak our truth, we are not being our authentic self. Speaking our truth does not necessarily mean being loud or boisterous. Speaking our truth conveys our authentic self to those around us, whether that is our students, administrators, family members, friends, etc.

Practice Reminder: "Today I will …"

Chapter 22
Voice

REFLECT

Here you have an opportunity to take some time and think about voice. You may find it beneficial to write out your responses.

- ❖ This chapter's Elevate quote is directly aligned to voice. Take a moment and read the quote aloud to yourself. See, hear, and feel the words. What resonates with you?
- ❖ Do I speak my truth?
  - ➢ If this is an area of growth for me, where will I start?
  - ➢ If this is an area of strength for me, how will I continue to grow?
- ❖ How do I speak my truth or use my authentic voice? To whom, in what situations or contexts, and where?
- ❖ What are some ways that I take care of my voice?
  - ➢ What are some ways that I take care of the physical aspects of my voice (such as drinking tea with lemon, not yelling, practicing voice exercises, resting, etc.)?
  - ➢ What are some ways that I take care of the emotional, social, and communicative aspects of my voice (such as sharing ideas with a trusted person, practicing assertiveness skills in front of a mirror, using positive self-talk, etc.)?
- ❖ If I haven't been practicing self-care for my voice, how will I start?
- ❖ Can I find opportunities to share the importance of finding and using my voice with others?

DISCOVER

If you want to explore this topic further, check out the resources below.

Places:

- Soulutions for Daily Living: https://soulutionsfordailyliving.com/?fbclid=IwAR1J4fOQ 3WE2TbYuSBL-KQgT9FBa5ky-d5nkxHgcbYx_qGkIbC2yNKZsdeo

Things:

- "How to Speak Your Truth," https://www.huffpost.com/entry/how-to-speak-your-truth_b_9565474
- "The Courage to Speak Your Truth ~ 5 Steps to Reclaiming Your Voice," https://www.vincegowmon.com/the-courage-to-speak-your-truth/
- "9 Easy Ways to Speak Your Truth Today," https://tinybuddha.com/blog/9-easy-ways-you-can-speak-your-truth-today/
- "6 Actionable Ways to Find and Speak Your Truth," https://www.mindbodygreen.com/articles/how-to-find-and-speak-your-truth

Chapter 23
Water

ELEVATE

> Chinese astrologers say that water is the most powerful element because it is perfectly nonresistant; when it is surging, water can sweep up everything in its way; over time, water can wear away the most solid rock. A heart full of love is just as strong.
> —Laura Bushnell, author

PRACTICE

Adult humans consist of about 60 percent water in total, with many of the specific organs and organ systems in the body being composed of 70 to 80 percent water. Water is a key element in our makeup as humans, more so than any other element in nature. Water connects us to nature and we cannot live without it. Adding water to your lifestyle, in many different ways, can make a tremendously positive impact. Drinking water regularly can improve so many bodily functions like increasing brain function, increasing energy level, relieving constipation, relieving headaches, aiding in weight loss, regulating body temperature, and more. Drinking water also has a healing component when a person is sick or feeling under the weather. Adding water to your everyday routine by taking a bath, making tea, or putting flowers around your house can provide comfort, joy, and an opportunity to wind down when stress is high. Many religions use water in their healing rituals.

Like humans, water is both versatile and powerful. Water can be gentle enough to clean a baby. Water can also be powerful enough to destroy a whole community or wear away a mountainside over time. As mentioned above, water is versatile and can be used in healing your body, mind, soul, and spirit. Water has the ability to refresh, renew, and recharge. Cultures around the world have been doing this for centuries. As educators, we barely get an opportunity to use the bathroom during the school day so drinking extra water throughout the school day may seem unrealistic. Think about how you can add more water into your daily routine, however that works best for you!

Practice Reminder: "Today I will …"

Chapter 23
Water

REFLECT

Here you have an opportunity to take some time and think about water. You may find it beneficial to write out your responses.

❖ This chapter's Elevate quote is directly aligned to water. Take a moment and read the quote aloud to yourself. See, hear, and feel the words. What resonates with you?

❖ How can I intentionally address my water intake?

❖ How can I continue to keep the importance of hydration in my daily plans?

❖ Water is fluid, flexible, creative, resilient, healthy, strong, and powerful. How can I celebrate these qualities in my water and in myself?

❖ Do I feel different or better when I'm fully hydrated?

❖ Many believe that water holds both a physical and spiritual quality. Do I have a strong connection to the ocean or bodies of water? Do I want to think or write about that?

❖ Many children and adults around the globe do not have easy access to pure water sources. Can I find ways today to be grateful for my easy access and abundance of water?

❖ Can I find opportunities to share the importance of water with others?

DISCOVER

If you want to explore this topic further, check out the resources below.

Things:

• *The Hidden Messages in Water* by Masaru Emoto

• Leech, J. (2017). 7 science-based health benefits of drinking enough water. https://www.healthline.com/nutrition/7-health-benefits-of-water

• "Life Source Water Systems: 7 Ways Water Can Improve Your Life," https://www.lifesourcewater.com/blog/self-care-7-ways-water-can-improve-your-life

• "Is Hydration One of Your Daily Priorities?" https://militaryfamilieslearningnetwork.org/2017/08/25/secrets-of-self-care-is-hydration-one-of-your-daily-practices/

• "We All Need Water for a Healthy Life – But How Much?" https://www.heart.org/en/news/2018/07/11/we-all-need-water-for-a-healthy-life-but-how-much

• "An Indigenous Approach to Healing with Water," https://upliftconnect.com/healing-with-water/

• "An Elemental Force of Healing – 3 Ways Water Heals," https://deborahking.com/an-elemental-force-of-healing-3-ways-water-heals/

• Ericson, J. 2013. "75% of Americans May Suffer from Chronic Dehydration, According to the Doctors." *Medical Daily.* https://www.medicaldaily.com/75-americans-may-suffer-chronic-dehydration-according-doctors-247393

• The National Academies of Sciences, Engineering, and Medicine. "Report Sets Dietary Intake Levels for Water, Salt, and Potassium to Maintain Health and Reduce Chronic Disease Risk." News release, February 11, 2004. https://www.nationalacademies.org/news/2004/02/report-sets-dietary-intake-levels-for-water-salt-and-potassium-to-maintain-health-and-reduce-chronic-disease-risk.

Chapter 24
RelaX

ELEVATE

> Successful teaching demands a level of commitment and emotional involvement that can be draining. I am convinced that finding time to relax, to focus on yourself, and things outside the job, is a key element in recharging those emotional batteries.
> —Penny Langfield, retired teacher

PRACTICE

Make relaxation a priority! You can read all the strategies, research, and anecdotal stories about the importance of relaxing and reducing stress, but none of that will work unless you make time to relax. How many times do you tell yourself or tell someone you love to "just relax," or say that you can't wait to go home and relax? It is time to take action. Before you can start to relax, you have to figure out what it means to relax for you and what activities you find most relaxing. This is a time of choice for you, and no one else. For example, during yoga the instructor directs the participants to bring their shoulders down away from their ears. In yoga, the participant might roll their shoulders back or intentionally relax the muscles in their neck or back to achieve this. To relax, you need to find what "brings your shoulders down," so to speak. When we are aware of how we are feeling, we can identify when we are in a tense or a relaxed state. Begin to notice when you are in a relaxed state. What are you doing? What are you feeling? Where are you? It may be a specific activity you enjoy or even a total lack of activity that brings you relaxation. Start by taking five minutes to do something (or nothing) that helps you to feel more relaxed. Then you'll slowly be able to take more and more time to relax. Relaxation is a habit that will serve you well. What you do to relax is a decision you must make for yourself.

Practice Reminder: "Today I will ..."

Chapter 24
RelaX

REFLECT

Here you have an opportunity to take some time and think about finding time to relax. You may find it beneficial to write out your responses.

- ❖ This chapter's Elevate quote is directly aligned to finding time to relax. Take a moment and read the quote aloud to yourself. See, hear, and feel the words. What resonates with you?
- ❖ What can I do to relax? What activities (or lack of activity) brings me joy?
- ❖ How much time can I devote each day or week to relaxing? How will I stick with it?
- ❖ How can I prioritize making time to relax?
  - ➢ What might I need to quit (see Chapter 17) to help me achieve this?
- ❖ Can I find opportunities to share with others about the importance of finding time to relax?

DISCOVER

If you want to explore this topic further, check out the resources below.

Things:

- "Stress Management: Relaxing Your Mind and Body," https://www.uofmhealth.org/health-library/uz2209
- "How to Relax: Tips for Chilling Out," https://www.healthline.com/health/stress/how-to-relax
- "How to Relax," https://www.headspace.com/meditation/how-to-relax
- "40 Ways to Relax: Beat Stress in As Little As 5 Minutes," https://greatist.com/happiness/40-ways-relax-5-minutes-or-less#Sip-and-nosh-your-way-to-relaxation-
- "How to Relax Your Mind and Body," https://www.verywellmind.com/how-to-relax-physically-and-emotionally-3144472
- "Creating the Habit of Not Being Busy," https://zenhabits.net/not-busy

Chapter 25
Yoga

ELEVATE

In the West, we view Yoga as a tool for flexibility and stress release. These are wonderful side effects of yoga, but not its primary goal. The goal of yoga is to go beyond our personalities, preference, beliefs, and conclusions to discover that we are something greater than the accumulations of the body and the mind. Thus, yoga is a path of ultimate expansion, where we expand ourselves beyond the boundaries of our identities to include and profoundly connect with all of existence.
—Henry Yampolsky, yoga instructor

PRACTICE

As educators, but more importantly as people, we need to connect. First, we need to connect with our own mind and body in order to care for ourselves in a meaningful way that allows us to, in turn, connect with our students and classrooms. There are many ways to build or improve your connection with yourself and others. Yoga promotes connecting with your mind and body, which is directly aligned with our mission. Yoga allows you time and space to connect with your mind by challenging you to put aside your worries, negativity, to-do lists, and errands and focus on the here and now. Yoga allows you time and space to connect with your body and your breath through movement. You may be able to notice where your muscles are feeling more tense or tight and you may be able to notice what movements bring about relief in those areas. The practice of yoga can be used in the classroom—maybe not directly, but indirectly, by putting aside your worries and to-do lists to focus on the present with your students or by listening to your body and how it responds to your environment or communicates your feelings with your students and colleagues. When you are aware of this connection, you can make small adjustments throughout the day to keep your flame bright.

Yoga can be a stand-alone strategy used for self-care. Yoga can also promote the use of multiple self-care strategies by providing the time and space to help educators practice or reflect on self-care strategies like breathing, gratitude, forgiveness, prayer, kindness, and awareness. During a yoga session, the instructor might encourage you to focus on your breath, think of what you are grateful for, or be kind to yourself on your yoga journey. During a yoga session, you might decide to forgive someone after releasing some of the tension in your muscles, or you might become more aware of an area of your body that needs more attention with stretching and movement. Yoga can help to facilitate many of the other strategies described in this book. Studies support that yoga can quite possibly decrease stress; relieve anxiety; reduce inflammation; improve heart health; improve the quality of life; fight depression; reduce chronic pain; promote quality sleep; and improve flexibility, balance, and strength.

Practice Reminder: "Today I will …"

Chapter 25
Yoga

REFLECT

Here you have an opportunity to take some time and think about yoga. You may find it beneficial to write out your responses.

- ❖ This chapter's Elevate quote is directly aligned to yoga. Take a moment and read the quote aloud to yourself. See, hear, and feel the words. What resonates with you?
- ❖ Have I tried yoga in the past? What was my experience?
  - ➢ Did it help reduce stress? Did it change how I was feeling afterward?
- ❖ Am I open to trying yoga for the first time or giving it a second chance?
  - ➢ If so, how can I get started?
- ❖ What barriers might be in the way for me to try yoga? Can any of those barriers be removed?
- ❖ Do I want to try yoga on my own or would it be helpful to try yoga in a group?
  - ➢ If I want to try yoga with others, is there someone in my circle (see Chapter 21) whom I can reach out to for support?
- ❖ Can I find opportunities to share the importance of movement and stretching with others?

DISCOVER

If you want to explore this topic further, check out the resources below.

Places:

- Yoga Breaks: https://kripalu.org/resources
- Yoga Digest: https://yogadigest.com/art-self-care-yoga/

Things:

- Ted talk with Henry Yampolsky: https://www.ted.com/talks/henry_yampolsky_what_motorcycling_in_the_himalayas_taught_me_about_connection_and_dialogue?fbclid=IwAR2wISszGwZrwBWXyXgXb63yClrYv5YEi5HIrLizsl7E9V7T5UlJjnYqOMA
- "The Yoga Journal:18 Reasons for Practicing Self-Care," https://www.yogajournal.com/lifestyle/18-reasons-to-practice-self-care/
- *The Yoga Diaries Stories of Transformation Through Yoga* – Editor Jeannie Page
- "15 Minute Gentle Yoga Routine for Self Care | Anxiety & Stress Relief," https://www.youtube.com/watch?v=WBeIDVpqKdY
- "Peaceful Practice: How Yoga Teaches us Self-Care," https://www.peacefuldumpling.com/peaceful-practice-yoga-teacher-self-care

Chapter 26
ExerciZe
/ˈeksərˌsīz/

ELEVATE

Teaching requires stamina. Physical exercise is as important as lesson planning!
—Lynn Trumbette, elementary assistant principal

PRACTICE

Do you wish there were more than twenty-four hours in the day because you want to find the time to exercise every day, but unfortunately, you just don't have the time? Do you then feel guilty because another day has gone by and you haven't exercised? Well, you are not alone.

"Exercise is just as effective as mindfulness at reducing people's stress and anxiety. … In most cases, mindfulness did positively impact anxiety, stress and depression, but there was no evidence it works better than exercise" (McGroarty, B., 2021). A good place to start is with an activity that you already enjoy or an activity you think you might enjoy. For Lauren, she fell in love with playing recreational coed football. It started as a way to make friends and eventually turned into the activity that Lauren looked forward to most throughout her week. Football gave Lauren the opportunity to be outside, interact with her peers, get in physical activity, build strength and endurance, and get out some of the frustration she was carrying with her. Once Lauren found football, making time to play didn't seem like just one more thing on her to-do list or just one more task to check off. Playing football was her time away to take care of her body through physical fitness, but it was also an opportunity to take care of her mind. At times, it was hard to find a babysitter or Lauren would have to cancel because one of her children was sick, but she always went back. Lauren was committed to her team and she was enjoying herself so it was much easier to "fit in." For Gerry, her activity is yoga. Yoga, like football, is easy to fit in because it doesn't feel like a chore or one more thing to do. What might it be for you? Maybe it is something you haven't tried yet or don't think you will enjoy.

Practice Reminder: "Today I will …"

Chapter 26
ExerciZe

REFLECT

Here you have an opportunity to take some time and think about exercise. You may find it beneficial to write out your responses.

- ❖ This chapter's Elevate quote is directly aligned to exercise. Take a moment and read the quote aloud to yourself. See, hear, and feel the words. What resonates with you?
- ❖ What types of activities do I already do?
  - ➢ If I don't do any, what might I enjoy doing?
  - ➢ What steps do I need to take to add a new exercise routine or physical activity?
- ❖ How do I feel in general about exercise?
- ❖ After trying exercise, have my feelings or opinions changed? Did I notice a positive *shift* in myself?
- ❖ Can I find opportunities to share with others about the importance of exercising?

DISCOVER

If you want to explore this topic further, check out the resources below.

Places:

- Fitness Blender: 600 Free Videos: https://www.fitnessblender.com/videos
- 25 YouTube Accounts to Follow for the Best Workout Videos: https://www.shape.com/fitness/workouts/10-best-workout-videos-youtube

Things:

- "Exercise," https://www.amherst.edu/campuslife/health-safety-wellness/counseling/self_care/exercise
- "Exercise for Self-Care," https://www.wellnesscorporatesolutions.com/exercise-for-self-care/
- "Self-Care: Why Exercise?" https://sova.pitt.edu/bepositive-self-care-why-exercise
- "Wellness Evidence Study: Exercise as Effective as Mindfulness at Reducing Stress," https://globalwellnessinstitute.org/global-wellness-institute-blog/2021/01/12/wellness-evidence-study-exercise-as-effective-as-mindfulness-at-reducing-stress/

Final Reflections

We need to celebrate what we have done, no matter how big or small the achievement. When we were younger we had definitive milestones, graduations, marriages, births, etc. As life progresses, things can be less defined. We can honor our own path by acknowledging, reflecting on, and appreciating what we've achieved during different chapters in our lives."
—Katie Slack, business consultant and life coach

Congratulations to you for completing your first round of *The Educator's Guide for Peace and Joy: An Alphabet of Strategies to Help You Light Your Inner Candle.* We powerfully pray that what you needed to find, learn, see, and do has been available specifically for you. Please be reminded that this book can be read and used in many different ways, and each time you read it or reread it, you have an opportunity to see, learn, and connect with the words and resources from a different viewpoint with a fresh perspective. We encourage you to revisit the quotes, the practices, the opportunities for reflection, and the myriad of resources available for you to dive into and discover.

Appendix

Blank Joy Inventory: Chapter 10 (Joy)

Daily/Regular Life Activities	Joy Score

Blank T-Chart: Chapter 12 (Love and Fear)

Love	Fear

Blank Nutrition Log: Chapter 14 (Nutrition)

Date: _____

Breakfast:

_____

_____

_____

_____

_____

Lunch:

_____

_____

_____

_____

_____

Dinner:

_____

_____

_____

_____

_____

Snacks:

_____

_____

_____

_____

_____

Thank You and Goodbye Box (TYG Box): Chapter 17 (Quit)

Comparing self to others	Excuses	Fixed Mindset	Perfectionism	Unhealthy foods
Living in the past	Addiction to social media	Multi-tasking	Need to control everything	Worrying about the future
Obsessing over little things	The need for approval	Resistance to change	Saying "yes" to everything and everyone	Going against your intuition
Unrealistic expectations of self	Thinking you have to do everything	Judging self and others	Need to impress others	Being busy 100 percent of the time
Negative people	Clutter	Complaining	Jealousy	Regrets
Adding debt	Criticism	Letting others make decisions for you	Discrediting yourself	Extra things, clothes, pounds
Defeating or negative self-talk	Multi-tasking	Unnecessary commitments	The need to always be right	Limiting beliefs
Comparing self to others	Excuses	Fixed Mindset	Perfectionism	Unhealthy foods

Suggested Further Reading

- Bernstein, Gabrielle. 2014. *May Cause Miracles: A 40-Day Guidebook of Subtle Shifts for Radical Change and Unlimited Happiness*. New York: Three Rivers Press.
- Brown, Brene. 2012. *Daring Greatly: How the Courage to Be Vulnerable Transforms the Way We Live, Love, Parent, and Lead*. New York: Avery.
- Brownstein, Ted. 2014. *The Interfaith Prayer Book*. Lake Worth, Florida: Lake Worth Interfaith Network.
- Bushnell, Laura. 2005. *Life Magic*. New York: Hyperion.
- Bushnell, Laura. 2001. *You Are a Rose*. United States: Magic Lady, Incorporated.
- Bushnell, Laura. 2014. *The Gift*. United States: Magic Lady, Incorporated.
- Dyer, Wayne Dr. 2012. *The Power of Intention: Learning to Co-Create Your World Your Way*. Carlsbad, California: Hay House, Inc.
- Emoto, Masaru. 2011. *The Hidden Messages in Water*. New York: Atria Books.
- Flor Rotne, Nikolaj and Didde Flor Rotne. 2013. *Everybody Present: Mindfulness in Education*. Berkeley, California: Parallax Press.
- Hanh, Thich Nhat. 1999. *The Miracle of Mindfulness*. Boston: Beacon Press.
- Hanh, Thich Nhat, Rachael Beresford, Paul Brion, and Katherine Weare. 2019. *Happy Teachers Change the World: A Guide for Cultivating Mindfulness in Education*. Old Saybrook, Connecticut: Tantor Media.
- Hay, Louise L. 1984. *You Can Heal Your Life*. Santa Monica, California: Hay House.
- Helmstetter, Shad, PhD. 1982. *What to Say When You Talk to Yourself*. New York: Pocket Books.
- Lindbergh, Anne Morrow. 1955. *Gift from the Sea*. New York: Pantheon.
- Mullings, Tamilla. 2020. *Becoming Me: 10 Ways to Affirm Self-Love*. Independently published.
- Northrup, Christiane, MD. 2020. *Women's Wisdom, Women's Bodies: Creating Physical and Emotional Health and Healing*. New York: Bantam Books.
- Russell, A.J. 2014. *God Calling*. Ulrischsville, Ohio: Barbour Publishing, Inc.
- Silva, Diana. 2017. *Molé Mama: A Memoir of Love, Cooking, and Loss*. San Francisco, California: CreateSpace Independent Publishing Platform.
- Wahba, Orly. 2017. *The Kindness Boomerang*. New York: Flatiron.
- Williamson, Marianne. 1996. *A Return to Love: Reflections on the Principles of "A Course in Miracles."* New York: HarperOne.
- Zupko, Corinne. 2018. *From Anxiety to Love: A Radical New Approach for Letting Go of Fear and Finding Lasting Peace*. Novato, California: New World Library.

References

- American Federation of Teachers & BATs. (2017). 2017 Educator Quality of Work Life Survey. Retrieved from: https://static1.squarespace.com/static/5d30f5468f2df10001eae004/t/5ddf2dba305b2260c9763c15/1574907324698/2017_eqwl_survey_web.pdf
- Canfield, J. (2017). How to create a vision board [video file]. Retrieved from: https://www.youtube.com/watch?v=iamZEW0x3dM
- Carver-Thomas, D. & Darling-Hammond, L. (2017). Teacher turnover: Why it matters and what we can do about it. Palo Alto, CA: Learning Policy Institute. Retrieved from:
- https://learningpolicyinstitute.org/product/teacher-turnover-report
- Collingwood, J. (2016). Learning to say no [webpage]. Retrieved from: https://psychcentral.com/lib/learning-to-say-no#1
- Dyer, W.D. (2005). The Power of Intention: Learning to Co-create Your World Your Way. New York, NY: Hay House Publishing, Inc.
- Greenberg M.T., Brown J.L., & Abenavoli R.M. (2016). Teacher Stress and Health. State College, PA: Pennsylvania State University. Retrieved from: https://www.rwjf.org/en/library/research/2016/07/teacher-stress-and-health.html
- Headspace. (2020). Breathing exercises to reduce stress [blog]. Retrieved from https://www.headspace.com/meditation/breathing-exercises
- International Council on Active Aging. (n.d.). The Seven Dimensions of Wellness [webpage]. Retrieved from: https://www.icaa.cc/activeagingandwellness/wellness.htm
- Mayo Clinic Staff. (2019). Stress relief from laughter? It's not a joke [webpage].
- https://www.mayoclinic.org/healthy-lifestyle/stress-management/in-depth/stress-relief/art-20044456
- National Institute on Aging. (n.d.). A good night's sleep [webpage]. Retrieved from: https://www.nia.nih.gov/health/good-nights-sleep
- National Wellness Institute. (2020).The Six Dimensions of Wellness Model [webpage]. Retrieved from: https://cdn.ymaws.com/members.nationalwellness.org/resource/resmgr/pdfs/sixdimensionsfactsheet.pdf
- Organization for Economic Co-operation and Development (OECD). (2017). "United States" in Education At a Glance 2017: OECD Indicators. Paris, France: OECD Publishing. DOI: http://dx.doi.org/10.1787/eag-2017-72-en
- Riser-Kositsky, M. (2019). Education Statistics: Facts About American Schools. Education Week. Retrieved from: https://www.edweek.org/leadership/education-statistics-facts-about-american-schools/2019/01.
- Souders, B. (2019). 24 forgiveness activities, exercises, tips, and worksheets [webpage]. Retrieved from https://positivepsychology.com/forgiveness-exercises-tips-activities-worksheets/
- TeachThought. (2019). A teacher makes 1500 educational decisions a day [webpage]. Retrieved from https://teachthought.com/pedagogy/teacher-makes-1500-decisions-a-day/
- The Project for Mental Health and Optimal Development (2020). Planning for uncertainty? An educator's guide to navigating the COVID-19 era [webpage]. Retrieved from: https://www.gse.upenn.edu/system/files/Planning-for-Uncertainty-Guide.pdf
- Weil, A. (2016). Three breathing exercises and techniques [webpage]. Retrieved from https://www.drweil.com/health-wellness/body-mind-spirit/stress-anxiety/breathing-three-exercises/

Other Resources

Mental Health Supports:

- "Common Myths & Misconceptions Debunked," https://www.talkspace.com/blog/what-i-wish-someone-had-told-me-about-how-therapy-actually-works/
- "A quick quiz to help people determine whether therapy might help them," https://psychcentral.com/quizzes/therapy-quiz/
- Psychology Today Extensive List of Therapists https://www.psychologytoday.com/us/therapists
- National Alliance on Mental Illness (NAMI) https://www.nami.org/Home

Mental Health Related Apps:

- eMoods: https://emoodtracker.com
- Mood-Log: https://apps.apple.com/us/app/mood-log/id730758811
- Moodtrack Diary: http://www.moodtrack.com
- https://www.wysa.ioWysa
- Daylio Journal - Self-Care Bullet Diary & Goals: https://apps.apple.com/us/app/daylio-journal/id1194023242
- Moodfit - Fitness for your Mental Health: https://www.getmoodfit.com/
- Talkspace - virtual therapy: https://www.talkspace.com/?_ga=2.27719796.915884614.1613677510-177462903.1613677510
- MoodMission: https://moodmission.com/
- Sanvello - self-care, peer support, coaching, therapy: https://www.sanvello.com/
- Headspace: https://www.headspace.com/
- Happify: https://www.happify.com/
- Shine - inclusive self-care tool kit: https://www.theshineapp.com/
- Breathe2Relax: https://apps.apple.com/us/app/breathe2relax/id425720246
- iCBT - identify, appraise, and reappraise negative thoughts: https://apps.apple.com/us/app/icbt/id355021834
- Calm - meditate, sleep, relax: https://www.calm.com/
- Youper - emotional health assistant: https://www.youper.ai/